Man the Tool-maker

Kenneth P. Oakley

Sixth Edition

Trustees of the British Museum (Natural History)
London: 1975

Publication No. 538
ISBN 0 565 00538 3
BMNH/50.75/20m/7/75

Printed in England by Staples Printers Limited at The George Press,
Kettering Northamptonshire

Preface to Sixth Edition

Research continues to add to the sum of our knowledge of the cultural activities of our early ancestors, and this new edition incorporates some of the most recent discoveries from the remarkable hominid sites in East Africa. Much interest has centred on the tool-making abilities of chimpanzees described by Jane Goodall; but as is pointed out by Dr Oakley, the perceptual motivation of apes is very different from the conceptual thinking of man, who is still supremely . . . the tool-maker.

H. W. BALL
Keeper of Palaeontology

April, 1972

Unless otherwise indicated, the specimens figured for the first time in this handbook, or without reference to published source, are in the collections of the Department of Palaeontology, British Museum (Natural History).

Contents

Man
the Tool-maker

1. Introduction

Man is a social animal, distinguished by "culture": by the ability to make tools and communicate ideas. Employment of tools appears to be his chief biological characteristic, for considered functionally they are detachable extensions of the forelimb. Other mammals have evolved specialized bodily equipment suited to some particular mode of life. Horses, for example, have teeth and hoofs suited to a plant-eating animal living on grassy plains; beavers are dependent for their way of life on incisor teeth capable of stripping and felling trees; the carnivorous sabre-tooth cats evolved claws like grappling irons and canine teeth like daggers, perfectly adapted for killing prey. In process of evolution man avoided any such specialization, and retained the pliant five-fingered hands which were so useful to his small tree-dwelling ancestors. When the immediate forerunners of man acquired the ability to walk upright habitually, their hands became free to make and manipulate tools—activities which were in the first place dependent on adequate powers of mental and bodily co-ordination, but which in turn perhaps increased those powers.

The evolution of new bodily equipment in response to a change of environment required millions of years, but relying on extra-bodily equipment of his own making, which could be quickly discarded or changed as circumstances dictated, man became the most adaptable of all creatures. Making fire, constructing dwellings and wearing clothes followed from the use of tools, and these cultural activities have enabled man not only to meet changes of environment, but to extend his range into every climatic zone.

While it is evident that man may be distinguished as the tool-making primate, it is questionable whether this definition gets to the heart of the difference between man and the higher apes. Structurally they are not very different; in fact they are classed by zoologists as members of the same group, the Hominoidea. Moreover, fossil primates transitional between apes and man are known. Sir Wilfrid Le Gros Clark, who made a special study of these transitional types (the australopithecines of Africa) said: "Probably the differentiation of man from ape will ultimately have to rest on a functional rather than on an anatomical basis, the criterion of humanity being the ability to speak and to make tools." This amounts to saying that the real difference between what we choose to call an ape and what we call man is one of mental capacity. It is worth considering the psychology of apes with this point of view in mind.

Observations of Professor W. Köhler, Madame Kohts and others on the habits of chimpanzees have shown that these apes are not only adept at learning by trial-and-error, but sometimes display remarkable insight. For example, Sultan, one of the male chimpanzees observed by Köhler, fitted together two bamboo tubes as a means of securing a bunch of bananas dangling beyond reach outside his cage; and on another occasion he attained the same end by fitting into one bamboo tube a piece of wood which he pointed for the purpose with the aid of his teeth. Apes are thus evidently capable of improvising tools. But it is important to note that the improvisations effected by Sultan were carried out with a *visible* reward as incentive. Köhler could obtain no clear indication that apes are ever capable of conceiving the usefulness of shaping an object for use in an imaginary *future* eventuality. He expressed this opinion:

"The time in which the chimpanzee lives [mentally] is limited in past and future. Besides in the lack of speech, it is in the extremely narrow limits in *this* direction that the chief difference is to be found between anthropoids and the most primitive human beings."

More recent observations have shown that the mental activities of chimpanzees are less limited than Köhler inferred, but still very limited in comparison with those of man. In 1960 Jane Goodall observed wild chimpanzees in Tanzania making simple tools, such as trimming selected grass blades or stems for use in fishing for termites in ant-hills (termitaries). Yet this is a far cry from the systematic making of stone tools, the earliest known examples of which (Figs. 16, 30) evidently required much premeditation, a high order of skill and an established tradition implying some means of communication.

Possession of a great capacity for conceptual thought, in contrast to the mainly perceptual thinking of apes and other primates, is now generally regarded by comparative psychologists as distinctive of man. The systematic making of tools of varied types required not only for immediate but for future use, implies a marked capacity for conceptual thought.

2. The Antiquity of Man

a. Early Controversies

If man is defined as the tool-making animal, then the problem of the antiquity of man resolves itself into the question of the geological age of the earliest known artifacts (objects deliberately shaped).

Until about 100 years ago the possibility that man had existed for more than a few thousand years had barely been considered. According to Archbishop Ussher's chronology which was still current the first man had been created in 4004 B.C. (on March 23rd according to a "Kalendar" of St John's College, Oxford). With the discovery of remains of mammoth and other extinct animals in the ancient river deposits (*Diluvium*) of various parts of Europe, the belief gained ground that there had been several periods of creation. Man, it was claimed, belonged to the last period, and the diluvial animals, or animals of the previous age, had been wiped out by a universal deluge of greater magnitude than the historic Noachian flood. The French palaeontologist Cuvier adhered to this view.

About 1690 a London pharmacist named Conyers found a pointed piece of flint close to the bones of an elephant unearthed in gravels near Gray's Inn Lane. He evidently recognized that this specimen was possibly an implement or weapon, for he preserved it, and a quarter of a century later an antiquary, John Bagford, illustrated and described it as "a British weapon made of flint lance like unto the head of a spear". Eighteenth century antiquaries readily explained how this specimen came to be associated with elephant bones; they said that it must have been the head of a spear used by a Briton in attacking one of the elephants which accompanied the Roman army under Claudius.

In 1797 another antiquary, John Frere, recognized as implements some chipped flints which had been found twelve feet below the surface in a brick pit at Hoxne in Suffolk, near Diss. He had genius enough to realize the implication of these finds, and published the view that they had been "used by a people who had not the use of metals", and belonged "to a very ancient period indeed, even before that of the present world".

The Gray's Inn Lane and the Hoxne implements (Fig. 18d) were in fact flint hand-axes—characteristic tools of the Early Stone Age—and they occurred in diluvial, or as we would now say, Pleistocene deposits. In the eighteenth century, however, the possibility of man's having an unrecorded prehistory was not exercising the minds of the learned (with one or two notable exceptions), and these discoveries attracted little attention. But in the early years of the nineteenth century the idea of man having a pre-diluvial origin was forming in the minds of several observers. Flint implements associated with bones of diluvial animals were reported from Belgian caves in 1832, and in 1840 from below a thick deposit of stalagmite in Kent's Cavern, Torquay. At this time orthodox scientists following Cuvier were incredulous of any such discoveries, and a fierce controversy developed when, towards the end of 1838, Boucher de Perthes, a French customs official and amateur archaeologist, announced that he had found in very ancient gravels of the Somme near Abbeville flints worked by "antediluvian" man. "In spite of their imperfection," he wrote (in 1846), "these rude stones prove the existence of man as surely as a whole Louvre would have done." He had been finding implements of the same type as those recognized earlier in England by Conyers and Frere, but the majority of scientists were very reluctant to accept his conclusions. However, in 1859 the English geologist Prestwich and the archaeologist John Evans visited Abbeville and investigated the evidence in detail. They returned convinced that Boucher de Perthes had found unquestionable proof of man's great antiquity.

Meanwhile geologists had been accumulating evidence that during the "diluvial" period ice-sheets spreading from highland areas had enveloped a large part of north-west Europe including much of the British Isles. The extinct mammoth (*Elephas primigenius*) and woolly rhinoceros (*Rhinoceros antiquitatis*), whose remains had been found in deposits of this age, were inhabitants of the sparsely wooded tundra which fringed the ice-sheets. In the eighteen-sixties excavations in the caves of south-western France brought to light skeletal remains of Ice Age man (at Cro-Magnon, Les Eyzies), as well as tools and pieces of bone and ivory on which he had carved pictures of the animals which he hunted, including mammoth, woolly rhinoceros and reindeer (Fig. 37).

As researches proceeded it became clear that the Pleistocene comprised an alternation of intensely cold or glacial, and warmer or interglacial periods, and that the Cro-Magnon cavemen lived during the last glacial, around 20,000 years ago, whereas the earliest hand-axes from the Somme gravels dated from a much earlier stage, when conditions were interglacial, and the fauna included hippopotamus and the straight-tusked parkland elephant, *Elephas antiquus*.

Within the present century it has been established that man existed in Europe during a temperate interval early in the Pleistocene Ice Age, about 400,000 years ago according to recent estimates.

b. The Problem of Eoliths

Although the oldest stone hand-axes dating from the earlier part of the Pleistocene are crude, they are nevertheless standardized tools, and this might suggest an immensely long tradition of slowly acquired skill. It has been thought unlikely that they are man's first efforts at tool-making, which were to be expected perhaps in the preceding Pliocene period.

Actual identification of man's earliest tools, however, is a matter of considerable difficulty, because obviously his first attempts at making tools from pieces of stone must have been all but indistinguishable from the accidents of nature. Indeed naturally fractured stones probably served as the first implements. Even at the present time there are tribes who make use of convenient bits of sharp stone, shark's

5

teeth and shells as tools. Some Australian tribes occasionally chop trees and fashion wooden implements with naturally shaped pieces of stone selected by virtue of their sharp cutting edges (Fig. 1).

Fig. 1. *Survival of "Eolithic" custom.* Aborigine of Pitjendadjara tribe, S Australia, cutting tree with an unflaked piece of stone which has a naturally sharp edge. *Photograph by C. P. Mountford, by courtesy of Royal Society of South Australia.*

The possiblity of discovering evidence of man in the Pliocene was being considered towards the end of the last century, and in 1891 Prestwich published an account of some crudely shaped flints, looking like simple tools (Fig. 2c) which had been found in patches of the "Pre-glacial" plateau drift on the North Downs of Kent by an amateur archaeologist, Benjamin Harrison, of Ightham. They became known as eoliths, since it was suggested that they were the earliest recognizable implements, and represented the dawn of tool-making (Greek, ἠώς = dawn, λίθος = stone). However, detailed studies have shown that all the Kent and Sussex eoliths can be matched exactly by stones chipped by natural agencies. Thus, any among them which have been chipped by man would not be distinguishable from the probably far greater number which have been shaped through the accidents of nature. The chief agency which has been responsible for the production of Kent eoliths appears to have been the powerful friction of one stone against another which occurs in soil-creep, particularly active under "periglacial" conditions (see p. 37, and Fig. 3*b*).

During the present century there has been a prolonged

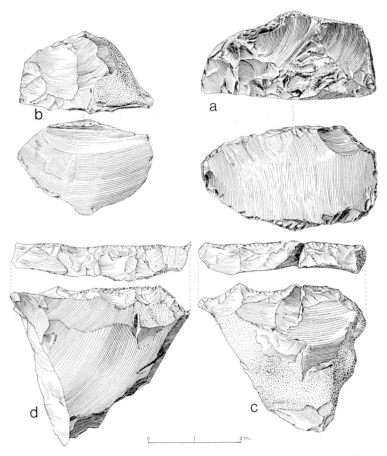

Fig. 2. *"Eoliths" and accidents of nature.* *a.* "Rostro-carinate" from base of Norwich Crag, Whitlingham. *After Ray Lankester.* *b.* Flint chipped by natural agency, below Eocene beds, Grays, Essex. *c.* Edge-chipped flint claimed by Benjamin Harrison as an "eolith". Plateau gravel, Ash, Shoreham, Kent. *d.* Flint with edges chipped by natural agency, below Eocene beds, Grays, Essex.

7

controversy regarding the human origin of chipped flints found in and below the shelly marine sands of East Anglia known as the Crags (this local name is derived from a Celtic word for shell). Although at one time the Crags were all regarded as Pliocene, the Red Crag, Norwich and Wey-bourne Crags are now classed as Lower Pleistocene (Villa-franchian stage). Most of the flints in question occur in the "Stone Bed" (Norfolk), or "Bone Bed" (Suffolk), which underlies the Crags. These sub-Crag eoliths include lumps of flint chipped into beak-shaped forms, or "rostro-carinates" (Fig. 2a), and flakes (Fig. 3c) with edges looking

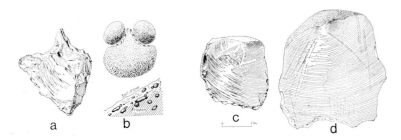

a   b   c   d

Fig. 3. *"Eoliths" and accidents of nature.* a. "Eolith" from river gravel at Pilt-down, Sussex. b. Diagram to illustrate how an "eolith" such as a could have been produced by soil-creep under periglacial conditions. c. Flint flake from Sub-Crag Stone Bed, West Runton, Norfolk. d. Flake of siliceous rock from glacial deposits of Permian age in South Africa. *After Breuil.*

as though they had been trimmed as scrapers. The chipping in some cases suggests intelligent design, but it is not possible to accept any of them unreservedly as the work of man, for it is known that similar forms can be produced by natural agencies, such as may conceivably have operated on flints in these beds (for example, friction between stones may have been engendered by the grounding of blocks of coastal ice in severe winters).

The problem of the antiquity of man the took-maker will hardly be affected by the outcome of the controversy about the East Anglian eoliths, for undoubted artifacts (pebble-tools) have now been found in several parts of Africa in deposits dating from the late Pliocene and earliest part of the Pleistocene indicating that humanity has been in existence for more than two million years.

Miocene and early Pliocene ancestors may have been tool-*users* without having reached the stage of systematic tool-making. It has been inferred that the immediate forerunners of man were able to live away from forests, in dry open country. They must have relied for defence on the use of improvised weapons—sticks or animal long-bones perhaps serving as clubs, and pebbles as missiles, while deliberate tool-making soon followed (p. 71).

c. Human and Natural Flaking Contrasted

It is convenient to consider here the various agencies in nature which cause flaking of stone, and to note the criteria by which human flaking can as a rule be distinguished from accidental.

Wherever it was available to him, Stone Age man made tools of flint or flint-like rock. Flint and similar hard homogeneous rocks break somewhat after the fashion of glass. A sharp blow directed vertically at a point on the surface of a slab of glass or flint knocks out a solid cone (resembling a limpet-shell in shape), with the apex or origin at the point of impact (Fig. 4a). Fracture of this type is called conchoidal (from κόγχη, Greek for shell). When a blow is directed obliquely near the edge of a slab of material which breaks conchoidally, a chip or *flake* is detached (Fig. 4b, b'). The fractured face of the flake looks like a mussel-shell; it has a half-formed *cone of percussion* at the point of impact, passing into a salient, or swelling, called the *positive bulb of percussion*, followed by low concentric ripples. There is a corresponding rippled hollow, or *flake-scar*, with *negative bulb of percussion*, on the parent lump, or core (Fig. 4c). The bulb of percussion on a large flake struck by a sharp blow commonly shows a miniature scar or *éraillure*, near the centre (Fig. 4b').

One of the chief accidental agencies by which stones are flaked is thermal change. Rapid changes of temperature cause unequal expansion or contraction of the surface of the stone or rock relative to its interior. In deserts, for example, the exposed surfaces of some types of rock are continually flaking as a result of the difference between the day and night temperature. In cold regions flakes are commonly split off by frost—the outer layer of the stone

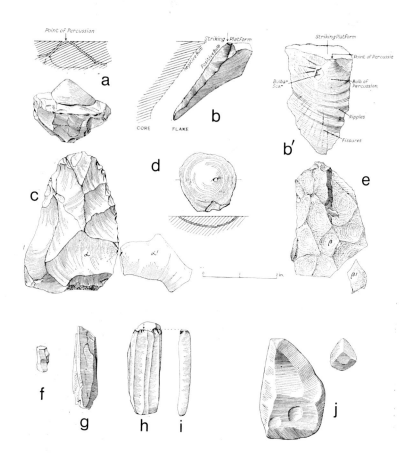

Fig. 4. *Characteristics of humanly worked flints, and natural forms sometimes mistaken for artifacts. a.* Complete cone of percussion in flint. *b, b′.* Flint flake struck by man (two views). *c.* Flint hand-axe (Palaeolithic core-tool), and one of the waste-flakes (α = flake-scar with negative bulb of percussion, α' = waste-flake with positive bulb). *d.* Rounded spall of flint ("pot-lid") split from nodule by frost action. *e.* Lump of flint pitted by the intersecting scars (*e.g.* β) of frost spalls (*e.g.* β'). *f.* Shrinkage-prism of starch. *g.* Flint showing prismatic-, or starch-fracture. *h.* Prismatic core of volcanic glass from which blades (such as *i*) have been struck; Chalcolithic, Crete. *j.* Ventifacts of dreikanter type: pebbles of jasper faceted by windblown sand; Carnac, Brittany.

expanding through the freezing of absorbed water. A flake or flake-scar due to frost or other thermal fracture is easily recognized, for the surface of fracture has either a roughish, blank appearance, or shows ripples concentric about a central point (the stresses set up by the thermal change being concentrated *within* the outer layer). On the other hand, the surface of a fracture due to a sharp external blow appears clean-cut, and shows a definite bulb of percussion with faint radial fissures and ripples originating at a point on the edge of the flake or flake-scar. Flakes split from a lump of flint by frost action are often round in outline and are commonly referred to as "pot-lids" (Fig. 4*d*). When the residual frost-pitted lump (Fig. 4*e*) happens to be of appropriate shape it is easily mistaken for an implement or weapon; but its natural origin is usually obvious on closer inspection. Thermal changes sometimes cause flint to break like starch, for example into prisms resembling blade cores (Fig. 4 *f–h*), but the lines of this form of thermal fracture have probably been determined in advance by strains set up by slow internal shrinkage. Stones splintered by fire, or faceted by sandstorms (ventifacts or dreikanters) are occasionally mistaken for the work of man (Fig. 4*j*).

Flakes struck by man show a well-defined bulb of percussion. The geologist H. B. Woodward remarked in 1878: "I was astounded to pick out of the stone bed of the Norwich Crag a flake containing a good bulb of percussion." He evidently believed that he was on the track of Pliocene Man. However, heavy stones hurled by the sea against flints firmly fixed in a beach commonly detach flakes showing bulbs; while bulbar flakes are produced also by the powerful pressure of one stone against another in a gravel which is disturbed by an overriding glacier, or by subsidence on a disintegrating bedrock, or by cliff-falls. But usually the flakes produced in such ways show flatter and more diffuse bulbs of percussion than those produced by purposeful blows.

A fair proportion of the flakes struck by man, even in primitive industries, have their edges dressed. But the edges of thin pieces of stone are very liable to become chipped through friction against other stones, such as occurs in soil-creep (solifluxion), in torrent action, or when stony deposits are caught up in the bottom layer of an ice-sheet.

As a general rule naturally chipped flints are easily distinguished from the works of man, for they lack logical design, flake-scars occur in uneconomical profusion, the edges have a bruised appearance, and the flake-surfaces are usually scratched. Frequently, also, there are signs (such as varying degrees of weathering or patination) that the flake-scars have been produced at several different dates. Nevertheless, under exceptional conditions naturally flaked stones occur which, if seen out of their geological context, might be mistaken for artifacts. For example, large numbers of broken flints with neatly chipped scraper-like margins occur in the Bullhead Bed under nearly 30 feet of Eocene sand at Grays in Essex (Fig. 2b, d). The flint nodules in this bed touch one another and they have been crushed together during the slow subsidence of the Eocene formation, which rests on a surface of Chalk which is undergoing solution. Again, stones flaked by glacial action into forms showing a remarkable resemblance to artifacts have been found in Pleistocene boulder clays, and in the Permian glacial beds of South Africa, some 180 million years old (Fig. 3d).

Thus, geologists are inclined to adopt a cautious attitude with regard to crudely chipped stones resembling artifacts, particularly if they occur in situations where natural flaking cannot be ruled out. By contrast even the most crudely chipped pieces of quartz found with the remains of Pekin Man in the Choukoutien caves can be accepted as implements merely on account of their situation (pp. 48, 72).

3. Origins of Tool-making

In the evolution of the primates the forelimbs have continually shown a tendency to take on functions performed in their ancestors and in other animals by the teeth. The use and manufacture of tools and weapons are an evident outcome of this tendency.

The apes of the present day are forest creatures subsisting mainly on plant and insect food, whereas all races of man of which we have knowledge generally include substantial amounts of animal flesh in their diet. It is suggested that some of the immediate ancestors of man lived in open grassland, and that they became addicted to eating raw flesh as a result of the struggle for existence being intensified by excessive drought. It may be recalled that baboons—monkeys that are mainly adapted to life on the ground—occasionally prey on lambs and other animals of similar size, using their powerful canine teeth as offensive weapons; and that this habit is liable to become more prevalent when conditions of existence are hard.

Man's ancestors lacked teeth suited to carnivorous habits, but they were ingenious, and hunting in hordes could easily have killed small and even some medium-sized animals, by cornering them and using improvised hand weapons, as they had perhaps learnt to do in the first place as a means of defence. But after the kill, removal of skin and fur often presented difficulty, which was overcome most easily by the use of sharp pieces of stone. Where no naturally sharp stones lay ready to hand, the solution surely was to break stones and produce fresh sharp edges. Once the tradition of tool-making had begun the manifold uses of chipped stones became obvious. They were useful for shaping sticks into spears sharp enough to be effective weapons in hunting the larger animals; for scraping meat from bones, for splitting them to get at the marrow, and so on.

It has been suggested that whereas flake-tools were devised for skinning animals, core-tools, such as "hand-axes" (see pp. 44-5), were intended for grubbing up edible roots, which probably formed an important element in the diet of Palaeolithic† and Mesolithic food-gatherers. However, Köhler's observations showed that even apes find no difficulty in digging things out of the ground with the aid of untrimmed sticks, casually picked up, and it seems more probable that hand-axes were primarily for cutting and scraping rather than for digging. Practical demonstrations by Dr L. S. B. Leakey and Dr A. J. Arkell have in fact proved that some forms of Acheulian hand-axe serve excellently for skinning game.

4. Materials used for Tools

a. Wood
The wooden implements of early man have rarely escaped

† For explanation of these and similar terms, see p. 91.

decay, except in water-logged deposits such as peat-bogs, and few of these are earlier than Mesolithic (Figs. 29*a*, 39). We may, however, infer the extensive use of wood in early Palaeolithic times from the frequency of "hollow" (*i.e.* concave) scrapers among the stone artifacts of that period. These scrapers probably served as spoke-shaves for the shaping of spears and the like. Only two wooden artifacts of early Palaeolithic age are known in Europe (but see p. 80). One is the end of a yew spear (Fig. 5) found in an interglacial peaty loam at Clacton-on-Sea. The other is a spear, also of yew wood but with fire-hardened tip, found with a skeleton of *Elephas antiquus* on a Levalloisian site at Lehringen, Saxony. Wooden artifacts have been found in waterlogged deposits of Lower Palaeolithic age in Africa. At Kalambo Falls, N. Rhodesia, digging sticks and a club were on an Acheulian living-site dated by radiocarbon as 57,000 years old (see also p. 80).

Australian aborigines use wooden spears and digging-sticks, with fire-hardened points; and they carve various articles (food-collecting bowls, shields, spear-throwers) out of lumps of wood laboriously hacked from trees with the aid of crude hand-choppers (Fig. 1). It is probable that many Palaeolithic tribes equipped themselves in comparable fashion, especially where soft woods were available. Trimmed boughs were possibly used for making windbreaks and other simple forms of shelter even in the earliest stages of culture. The introduction in Neolithic times of the polished stone axe-head, capable of producing broad clean cuts, led to greater precision in the working of wood, and to its use on a large scale in the construction of dwellings.

b. Bone

The use of bone for tools dates from the beginnings of human activity, in fact it probably followed quite naturally from the hunting of animals as a source of food. Animal bones broken for the extraction of marrow are common in deposits formed on the dwelling sites of Stone Age man, and suitably shaped pieces of bone would have been selected by him for use at least as occasional tools. Where easily flakeable stone was scarce, bone was probably used extensively by early man. In the Choukoutien cave deposits

cm in

Fig. 5. *Working of wood.* Wooden spear and flint "spoke-shave" from Palaeolithic deposit, Clacton-on-Sea, Essex.

there were found associated with the remains of Pekin Man numerous pieces of broken bone, apparently used as tools (Fig. 6*a*, *b*).   It is difficult to *carve* bone with a flint

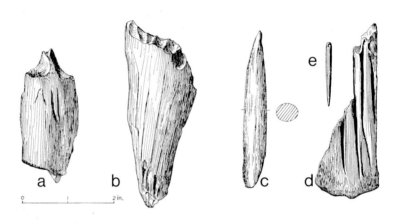

Fig. 6.   *Working of bone and antler.   a, b.* Broken animal bones chipped for use as tools, "*Sinanthropus*" deposits near Pekin.   *After Breuil.   c.* Awl of polished antler, Upper Palaeolithic, Torbryan caves, Devon.   *d.* Cannon-bone of horse from which slivers of bone have been gouged out for needles, Magdalenian, Grotte des Eyzies (Dordogne).   *e.* Polished bone needle, Magdalenian, Bruniquel caves (Tarn-et-Garonne).

knife, and in early Palaeolithic times bones were converted into tools mainly by breaking and chipping.   In the later Palaeolithic, man learnt that he could shape bone, antler and ivory by a combination of gouging, sawing, splitting, scraping and rubbing on an abrasive stone (Figs. 6*c–e*, 35). Antler proved to be more easily carved, after the manner of wood.   The Cro-Magnons and related races of *Homo sapiens* living in the open, almost treeless tundra of Europe made extensive use of reindeer antler and mammoth ivory, as well as of bone, shaping and engraving these materials with remarkable artistry (Figs. 25, 27).

Since bone substance disintegrates fairly quickly in acid soils, Palaeolithic implements of bone and related materials have only survived in calcareous sands, limestone gravels and cave-deposits.

c. Shell

For special purposes, or where stone is scarce, strong shells have occasionally been used as material for primitive tools. The Neolithic Egyptians made fish-hooks from the shell of the Nile oyster, *Aetheria*. The Pre-Caribs of Barbados made celts from the shell of a large marine gastropod, *Strombus gigas*. In Micronesia adze-blades are still made of *Tridacna* shell.

d. Stone

Human progress has gone step by step with the discovery of better materials of which to make *cutting* tools, and the history of man is therefore broadly divisible into the Stone Age, the Bronze Age, the Iron Age, and the Steel Age (Fig. 7). These are stages of technical development, rather than

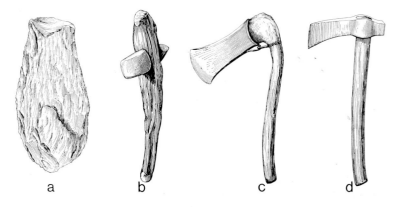

a   b   c   d

Fig. 7. *Progress in axes. a.* Chipped stone axe (cleaver) for use in hand, Palaeolithic, Kenya, × ⅙. *b.* Polished stone axe-head (celt) in wooden haft, Irish peat bog, × ¼. *After Wilde. c.* Socketed bronze axe-head on wooden shaft, salt-mine, near Salzburg, Austria, × ⅙. *After Montelius. d.* Iron axe-head (handle reconstructed), Roman, × 1/12. *After Collingwood.*

chronological periods. Thus the Stone Age, which dawned with man himself three or four million years ago, ended in the Middle East with the discovery of metals about 4000 B.C., but Stone Age culture persisted until after 2000 B.C. in Britain, and in parts of Australia has lasted until the present day.

Man soon learnt that some kinds of stone are better than

others for chipping into tools, and wherever they were available he chose siliceous rocks and minerals with perfect conchoidal fracture, namely, flint, chert, obsidian, chalcedony and fine-grained silcretes. These forms of silica are very hard, yet they can be chipped or flaked quite easily, giving a fractured edge as sharp as a razor. In Europe, particularly in England and France, flint was the rock most commonly used by prehistoric man for making into implements.†

Flint occurs in the Chalk as layers a few inches thick (tabular flint) or as rows of scattered nodules (Fig. 8).

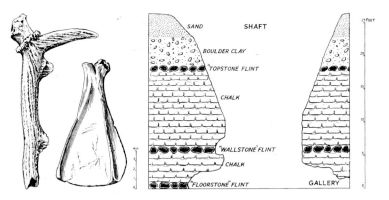

Fig. 8. *Flint mining. On right:* Section of Neolithic mine at Grime's Graves, Norfolk. The Floorstone is tabular. *On left:* Tools used by Neolithic and Bronze Age miners: shoulder-blade of ox used as shovel, Harrow Hill, Sussex (*after Curwen*); red-deer antler pick, Grime's Graves.

Where the Chalk has been worn away by the natural agencies of denudation, flint, being hard and resistant to weathering, has been left behind in the form of gravel or shingle.

Flint consists of minutely crystalline silica (mineralogists describe it as microcrystalline quartz). In broken, unweathered pieces it is glossy and appears black, grey or brown—very thin pieces are translucent. Nodules fresh from the Chalk, or from the residual formation called Clay-with-flints, generally show a dull white outer crust

† In the illustrations of this handbook all the flaked stone artifacts from Europe are of flint unless otherwise stated.

or cortex. The difference between the white cortex and the glossy, relatively dark interior of a flint nodule is one of texture only; the cortex is porous and scatters light, while the interior is very dense in structure and absorbs light. Flint has ultra-microscopic pores which are enlarged by the action of various natural solvents, so that when pieces of the typical dark flint are weathered they develop a porous skin or patina. Initially this appears bluish or white (depending on the depth to which weathering has proceeded), but it is apt to become stained yellowish-brown or red through absorbing iron compounds from percolating water.

In the Palaeolithic and Mesolithic periods man obtained flint mainly from the banks and beds of rivers or from cliffs and sea-beaches. In the Neolithic stage he learnt to follow good quality flint underground, and sank mines into the Chalk in search of it (Fig. 8). At Grime's Graves, near Weeting in Norfolk, and at Cissbury and Harrow Hill in the South Downs of Sussex, the Neolithic and Bronze Age miners dug shafts up to 40 feet deep to reach the best seams of flint, which they worked by means of galleries. They used picks and wedges made out of red-deer antler, and in Sussex, shovels made out of shoulder-blades of oxen. Similar flint mines, also dating from the second millennium B.C., have been found at Spiennes in Belgium, and in Sweden, France and Portugal. Only seams of the highest quality were worked, others of equal thickness but slightly inferior texture being neglected. The fine honey-coloured flint of Le Grand Pressigny (Indre-et-Loire) was traded as far as Switzerland and Jersey.

Siliceous stone similar to flint, but originating in rock formations other than Chalk, is generally called *chert*. Thus there are cherts in the Carboniferous Limestone of Derbyshire and West Yorkshire, in the Portland Beds of Dorset and in the Upper Greensand of Dorset and Devon (Fig. 23g), all of which were used by early man. Sometimes the term flint is applied to any siliceous stone whose quality is the same as that of typical Chalk flint, the name chert then being restricted to coarse-grained types. Egyptian "flint" (Figs. 12b, d, 40b) is identical in quality with Cretaceous flint, although derived from Eocene limestone.

In some regions, for example in Burma and the Sudan, Palaeolithic man made implements of silicified wood, which

19

has a flint-like consistency, but flakes easily in one direction only (Fig. 20*f*). Elsewhere he occasionally used pure chalcedony (Fig. 12*g*), a mineral deposited by siliceous solutions, for example in hollow flints and in the steam cavities of lava. This material is usually translucent and bluish-white, but may be red (when it is known as cornelian). Red or yellow opaque forms of chalcedony are called jasper.

The Australian aborigines discovered in modern times that bottle-glass and porcelain telegraph insulators serve as excellent materials for making spearheads (Fig. 12*h*). In a few regions early man used the shiny black volcanic glass called obsidian, which has a perfect conchoidal fracture and was deemed to be even superior to flint for flaking into tools and weapons (Figs. 4*h*, *i*, 29*c*, *d*). Obsidian appears greenish or grey by transmitted light, and in very thin pieces is transparent. It occurs in the Admiralty Islands; in Mexico, where the Aztecs made mirrors of it; in Kenya, where it was mined by late Palaeolithic Caspians; in the Island of Melos in the Aegean, at Kaisarieh in Turkey and by Lake Van in Armenia. Obsidian was so highly valued, particularly for the production of blades, that it became an object of trade in Neolithic times. About 3500 B.C. there was a village near Lake Van housing a community employed on quarrying obsidian for export to Syria and elsewhere. Yellow-green glass of possibly extra-terrestrial origin in the Libyan Desert was used by the Late Palaeolithic Aterians.

In parts of the world where Archaean and crystalline rocks predominate, flint and flint-like materials are generally lacking. In these regions tools were often made of quartz, a crystalline form of silica occurring in veins connected with granites. The clear variety (rock-crystal) has been prized by man since the earliest times, presumably on account of its attractive appearance. Flawless crystals fracture conchoidally and serve for small tools, but are rare (Fig. 31*e*). The commonly used white vein-quartz, consisting of crystals matted together, breaks irregularly, and is a most difficult stone to work. Other rocks used by Stone Age man included sandstone hardened by secondary silica (silcrete or sarsen), recrystallized sandstone (quartzite), siliceous slate (lydian stone), ironstone, volcanic rocks, such as basalt, rhyolite or phonolite lava (Fig. 18*a*), and intrusive igneous rocks of even grain such as diorite. The fracture of these close- or medium-grained kinds of stone approaches the conchoidal, but the bulb of percussion is less pronounced than in flint. Ridges and grooves radiating from the point of percussion form a more evident feature of the surface of a humanly-struck flake in such materials (Fig. 22g).

In the Palaeolithic stages of culture, when almost all stone artifacts were shaped by processes of flaking, flint and similar siliceous rocks were obviously the ideal tool materials, and even slightly coarser-grained rocks were poor substitutes. However, at the end of the Stone Age, in the Neolithic stage (and locally even in the Mesolithic), when men learnt to shape stone tools by grinding instead of chipping, they found that they could make effective use of rocks such as basalt and diorite which had relatively poor conchoidal fracture; and even chose them in preference to flint for making some classes of tool, such as celts (stone axes, adzes or hoes wielded by a shaft), where toughness and a readily ground edge were important requirements. The qualities of certain rocks, of proved or imagined worth, were keenly appreciated by the makers of celts in Neolithic times. Green rocks appear to have been favoured. A greenish, close-grained lava (technically called augite-granophyre) outcropping at Graig Lwyd on Penmaenmawr, North Wales, was specially popular. The site where the axe-heads were chipped into rough shape has been found on the mountainside (Fig. 13d). It is possible that the final grinding and polishing was done on the sea-shore. Other Neolithic axe-factory sites have been found at Stake Pass and Pike of Stickle in the English Lake District, where grey-green volcanic tuffs of restricted occurrence were used. Axes of these special rocks were traded widely, even into areas where axes of local flint were in common use. Thus celts of Graig Lwyd rock have been identified as far east as the Cambridge Fens, and of Stake Pass rock (andesite tuff) as far south as Surrey and Southampton. Axe-heads of "greenstone" (epidiorite) were traded widely from Cornwall in Neolithic and Bronze Age times, while finely polished celts of the vivid green mineral jadeite were occasionally exported to Britain from Brittany, probably for ceremonial use.

e. Metal

A very long interval elapsed between the discovery of metals and their general utilization as tool materials in place of stone. It appears that copper was the earliest metal to become known. Since it is not found in a pure state in the region where it first came into use, some accidental smelting of the common green ore, malachite, most probably led to the discovery of this metal. In recent years prospectors at Katanga in the Belgian Congo reported seeing bright globules of copper among the charcoal fires lit by Africans close to pieces of cupriferous rock. In some such way early man presumably first encountered copper. Its bright appearance would attract him, and he would find it could be hammered into desired shapes. The earliest known metal artifacts are beads and pins of beaten copper found in Badarian graves in Egypt, dating from about 4000 B.C. At first men shaped this new material by beating it in the cold state, as though it were some form of stone, and at this stage there was a tendency simply to copy the old types of stone tools and weapons in copper. Before long, however, it was realized that copper when molten can be *cast* into any required shape, that it hardens on cooling, and can then be given a fine edge which is durable. This discovery led to the introduction of new types of tool and to revolutionary advances in culture. Presumably, as soon as man became awake to the value of metal for making tools, and saw the possibility of transmuting stones into metals, he experimented with any rocks which appeared promising. At any rate, soon after 3000 B.C. metal workers in Mesopotamia were evidently familiar with tin, and had found that by mixing it with copper they could produce a new metal—the alloy bronze—which could be cast more easily and which made better cutting tools.

In Europe both copper and bronze long remained scarce commodities reserved mainly for special weapons and ornaments. Copper tools and weapons were being made on a limited scale in south and central Europe around 2000–1800 B.C., but stone artifacts predominated, and culture elsewhere in Europe was still essentially Neolithic. It is interesting to note that the flint daggers (Fig. 12a) made in Denmark during the transitional period (sometimes called the Aeneolithic or Chalcolithic) were imitations of imported copper ones. In the north, stone axes, flint arrowheads and scrapers (Fig. 12e, f) continued in common use throughout most of the Bronze Age—and even later in remote districts.

Iron of meteoric origin was occasionally used for making beads during predynastic times in Egypt. Smelting of iron ore for the manufacture of tools and weapons began in Asia Minor soon after 1300 B.C., but the regular use of iron did not spread to Western Europe until nearly 500 B.C. Although the rise of modern industrial civilization depended largely on the harnessing of newly discovered sources of power, it owed much to the introduction of a wide range of steel alloys for making cutting tools—carbon-steel, manganese-steel and so on.

5. The Making of Stone Implements

Before describing the succession of Stone Age industries in relation to man's evolutionary development, which is the central theme of this handbook, it is useful to consider the various ways in which stone can be worked into tools and weapons. The simplest way of producing a stone which will cut (the primary type of artifact) is simply to break it in half and to use the resulting fresh sharp edge; but to produce a stone tool which is even slightly more specialized, one of two courses must be followed. The lump of stone, whether pebble, nodule or angular fragment, can be brought to the desired shape by flaking, or knapping. The flakes removed from the lump are then primarily waste-products, while the core of the lump becomes the implement. Such is a *core-tool* (Fig. 4c). Alternatively, flakes struck from the lump can be used as implements, with or without further trimming (known as dressing, retouch or secondary work). In this case the core is the source of *flake-tools* (Fig. 4b), and will serve to yield flakes until too small, when it is discarded as waste. Before a core will yield flakes of the required shape it may have to be prepared, and in the course of the preliminary work a number of waste flakes are produced. In practice, too, the flakes removed in the production of a core-tool may be selected subsequently for use as implements. The simple classification into core-tool industries and flake-tool industries is further complicated by the possibility that large flakes may be selected to serve as cores.

23

Moreover, even in a flake-tool industry, discarded cores would be used as occasional tools (*e.g.* Fig. 21*a*).

Industries producing long parallel-sided flakes are distinguished as *blade-tool* industries (Fig. 24). (It is difficult to produce blades in rocks other than flint, chert or obsidian.)

There are several methods of flaking stone, each probably used at some time or other during the Stone Age. Flaking by direct blows with a hammerstone (or other tool for striking) has been the method most widely used, but even this is subject to considerable variation. The stone to be flaked can be held in the hand (Fig. 11*a*), or rested on a block, or held against the knee. If, while it is being struck, the stone is rested on a slab of rock (a technique reminiscent of the simple method of cracking nuts with a pebble), the resulting flakes are liable to show a bulb of percussion at both ends, owing to rebound from the anvil. This so-called bipolar technique was practised by Pekin Man (Fig. 31*d*). The normal primitive method of knapping, however, is to hold the lump of stone to be flaked in the hand, and to strike it repeatedly at selected spots with a pebble of suitable size. Each blow is delivered obliquely downwards near the edge of some conveniently placed flattish area (the striking platform), usually the scar of a flake previously struck off. Whether the flakes are short and thick, producing step-like bites along the edge of the piece of stone, or whether they are thin and extensive, skimming the surface, depends largely on the placing of the blows and on the angle at which they are delivered. The run of the flake can be controlled by preparation of the face of the core, and also by pressure of the finger. When a piece of stone is held in the hand and struck at the edge by blows directed obliquely downwards, the flakes come off the *lower* surface, against which the fingers or palm are easily pressed. In the shaping of a core-tool such as a hand-axe, which requires to be trimmed equally on two sides, it is turned over from time to time as the paring proceeds.

Experiments by the French master mason, Léon Coutier, have shown that flint and similar rocks can be flaked by direct blows with a bone or cylindrical bar of hardwood. This is an effective way of reproducing the smooth skimming flake-scars which form the surfaces of the finer palaeoliths (Fig. 18). Similar flake-scars, with subdued or soft bulbs of percussion, can be produced also by a cylindrical hammer-stone, especially if used in conjunction with skilful finger control.

Probably one of the most primitive methods of producing flakes for use as tools is to dash or swing the core against the edge of a larger stone, or anvil. This "block-on-block" technique is liable to produce thick flakes (and keep flake-scars on the core) as in coarse flaking by a hammerstone, but

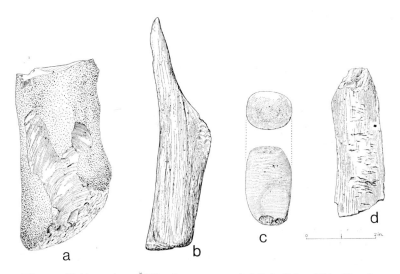

Fig. 9. *Flaking tools. a.* Flint hammerstone (2¾ lb.), Palaeolithic (Leval-loisian), Northfleet, Kent. *b.* Antler tine used for pressure-flaking, Neolithic or Bronze Age, Harrow Hill, Sussex. *After Curwen. c.* Sandstone hammer-stone (3 oz.), probably Bronze Age, Santon Warren, Norfolk. *d.* Bone com-pressor or anvil, Mousterian, La Quina (Charente).

with more protuberant cones and bulbs of percussion, and with a wider flaking angle (the angle between the striking-platform and the surface of the bulb of percussion—see Fig. 4*b*, *b'*). Flakes belonging to the primitive Palaeolithic flake industry known as Clactonian show these features (Fig. 21*c*).

A common attitude of a stone knapper is a sitting or squatting one, and in the production of flake-tools by per-cussion with a hammerstone the core is generally held on the left thigh or knee. The knapper starts as a rule with a lump of stone far larger than the core or tool required. Experiments have shown that the preliminary trimming down and the production of large primary flakes are most easily accomplished with a hammerstone weighing about 3 lb., whereas for the subsequent dressing of flakes a hammerstone weighing 2 or 3 oz. gives the best results (Fig. 9a, c).

It is interesting to consider the procedure of the flint-knappers of Brandon, Suffolk, who still make gun-flints for

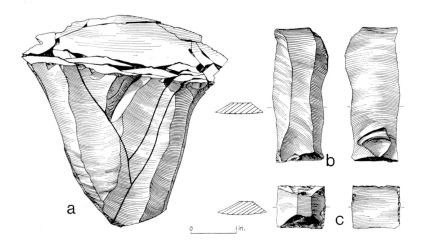

Fig. 10. *Manufacture of gun-flints. a.* Flint core with blades replaced, Brandon, Suffolk. *b.* Blade ready for division into gun-flints, Icklingham, Suffolk. *c.* Brandon gun-flint (horse-pistol).

export to the U.S.A. and to the natives of West Africa at the rate of 15,000 a month.

A Brandon knapper takes a large nodule of good quality dry flint, usually weighing at least ¼ cwt., places it on his knees and divides it into four by means of a 5 lb. steel-faced hammer. There are planes of weakness in nearly all rocks, even those as homogeneous as flint, and the experienced flaker takes advantage of this. The knapper, tapping the flint with his heavy hammer, knows by the ring where to strike, and a lunge from his elbow generally suffices to make the hammer split the huge nodule along a line of weakness. Taking a light hammer of different pattern, he holds one of the quarters on his padded knee, and using one of the freshly cleaved faces as a striking-platform, strikes off a series of long parallel-sided flakes from the sides of the quarter until it becomes a fluted cone (Fig. 10a). The second set of blades is struck from the core in such a way that each includes a pair

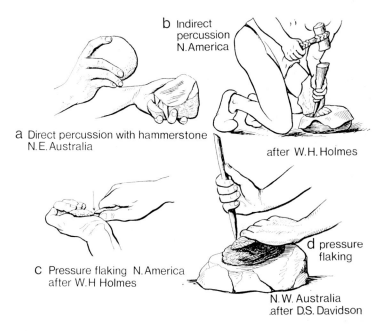

Fig. 11. *Methods of flaking stone.*

of the ridges left by the previous round of flaking. In this way broadly bevelled blades of the required size are produced (Fig. 10b), which can be divided and trimmed into sharp-edged rectangles (Fig. 10c) to fit the striker of a flint-lock gun or pistol. The division and trimming of the gun-flints is done with a specially shaped light hammer on a small steel anvil (set in a bole of wood). The standard sizes are musket, carbine, horse-pistol, large gun, small gun and pocket-pistol. The extreme precision with which these gun-flints

27

are turned out depends partly on the knapper being a highly skilled craftsman, but also on the use of a series of steel hammers, each tool being of standardized pattern.

Stone Age knappers relied wholly on craftsman's skill, and when they required flakes of standard type or long blades, they had to take great care in the preparation of the core. Studies of the flaking techniques employed by primitive peoples in recent times show that there are many different ways of producing the same result. The American Indians used various methods of indirect percussion. To produce blades, for instance, a wooden or bone punch was interposed between the hammerstone and the core (Fig. 11b). Owing to the reduction of shatter, flakes can be split off thus with greater precision than when the hammerstone is used directly. The Aztecs of Mexico and a few North American Indians produced long blades by what is called impulsive pressure. The core was stuck in the ground and gripped by the feet of the flaker, who either stood or sat, and grasped a wooden staff, which had a cross-piece for resting against the chest, and spike of a horn or hardwood at the other end which was set on the prepared edge of the core. The flaker would thrust forward with his chest, thus using the leverage of the body to split a flake from the core. According to one seventeenth century observer, a Mexican flaker, using this method, could produce as many as 100 knife blades of obsidian in an hour.

Much has been learnt about the more primitive flaking techniques by studying the methods of Australian aborigines. As a general rule the shaping of a core-tool takes only a few minutes, but the preparation of a core for the production of flake- or blade-tools is sometimes a lengthy proceeding. Moreover, a number of artifacts are rejected before completion. It has been stated that in North Queensland, for example, a native requiring a new knife will visit a traditional quarry and will perhaps strike as many as 300 flakes before he obtains what he considers to be a suitable blade. The rejects and waste-flakes are left on the working "floor" (Pl. II, 2), while the single satisfactory blade is taken away, mounted in a handle of resin and used until it is broken. The dressing, or secondary working of a stone tool to make the edge straighter or more serviceable, or to re-edge it when it has been blunted by use, is usually done by rapping it on a pebble, or with a piece of bone or hardwood. Some of the tribes, especially in the Kimberley region of Western Australia, dress spearheads by pressure-flaking.

According to first-hand accounts of the fashioning of a spearhead by this method, a flake of stone (or glass, or porcelain) is taken and its edges chipped with a hammerstone into a roughly symmetrical leaf form. The margins are then rasped with a piece of sandstone, which breaks away small chips so that a narrow platform or bevel is formed on each side of the edge. The completion of the spearhead by pressure-flaking requires much patience and skill. The native squats on one heel, with the other leg stretched out, and with an anvil stone on the ground between his legs. In his left hand he holds the unfinished spearhead on a cushion of paperbark, placed on top of the anvil stone. In his right hand he holds a pointed stick of hardwood (or piece of kangaroo bone), in such a way that the sharpened end is close to the wrist and points towards his body. After adjusting the point of the stick against the bevel of the far edge of the flake, he brings the weight of his body to bear on his right arm, and at the same time levers his wrist downwards and outwards. A chip snaps off the lower surface of the flake, while the "jar" of the downward thrust is absorbed by the cushion (Fig. 11d). The process is repeated time after time, as he works along the edge towards the butt; then the flake is reversed and the same method applied to the other side. A skilful flaker can make a spearhead of bottle-glass in about ten minutes.

The Mousterians and Upper Palaeolithic peoples commonly used pressure against a bone for the edge-trimming of flakes and blades (Fig. 9d). Most of the finer stone implements of the Neolithic and Bronze Ages, such as arrowheads (Fig. 12c–f), were finished by pressure-flaking, probably of the type employed by American Indians (Fig. 11c). Experiments have shown, however, that in the case of flint it is practically impossible to detach spalls more than half an inch in length by simple pressure. Glass and obsidian are more amenable to this method of flaking, but flint artifacts surfaced by long parallel flutings, such as the larger Solutrean laurel-leaf points (Fig. 26d), Egyptian flint knives (Fig. 12b) and Danish flint daggers (Fig. 12a), were probably flaked by indirect percussion, perhaps by use of bone or wooden

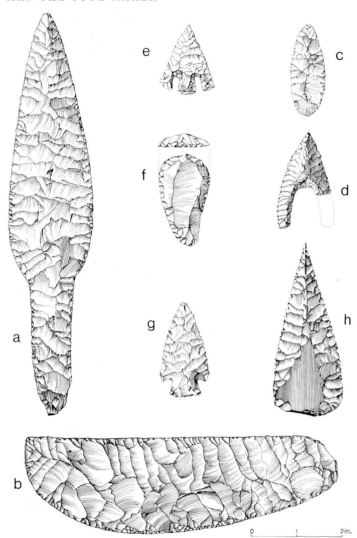

Fig. 12. *Examples of pressure-flaking and indirect percussion.* *a.* Flint dagger Chalcolithic, Denmark. *b.* Flint knife, Pre-dynastic, Egypt. *c.* Leaf-shaped arrowhead, Neolithic long-barrow, Levisham Moor, Yorkshire. *d.* Concave-base flint arrowhead, Neolithic, Fayum, Egypt. *e.* Barbed and tanged arrow-head, Bronze Age, Lakenheath, Suffolk. *f.* End-scraper, Bronze Age "floor", Cavenham Heath, Suffolk. *g.* American Indian arrowhead (chalcedony). *h.* Australian (Kimberley) spearhead of bottle-glass.

punch in combination with hammerstone or mallet (Fig. 11b).

The methods of working stone so far described are all methods of flaking, and as such are well adapted for making knives and scrapers and spearheads. Crude axe-heads also can be chipped out of stone, but even the most refined flaking technique fails to give the smooth-faced cutting edge required to make an adze- or axe-head effective in the felling of trees and in the working of wood on a scale large enough for making boats and dwellings. Man's eventual need of effective axes, adzes and chisels was met by a revolution in tool-making which took place during the Mesolithic stage of culture. The technique of grinding and polishing, already applied to bone and ivory in late Palaeolithic times, began to be used also for the edging and eventually for the surfacing of stone tools. It is not known if the idea of grinding stone axe-heads arose in response to like needs in several regions simultaneously, or if it originated in one place and was passed on through tribal contacts. But within a few thousand years ground or polished stone axe-heads were being used over a large part of the inhabited world.

The finer-grained igneous rocks, such as basalt and epidiorite (greenstone), lend themselves to grinding and polishing more readily than flint. It seems probable that the new technique was first adopted in regions where such rocks were being used as tool-materials in place of flint. The earliest known axe-heads with ground edges are made from water-worn pebbles of fine-grained rock, and are associated with a Mesolithic flint industry in Sweden dating from about 6000 B.C. However, it was with the spread of the Neolithic practice of agriculture, starting in the Near and Middle East at about this date, that the use of polished stone axe- and adze-heads (celts) became general. It is probable that one of their main uses was for felling small trees and working wood. They were entirely superseded by copper and bronze celts in the prosperous centres of civilization in the Middle East around 3000 B.C., but continued to be used in barbaric Europe until the end of the Bronze Age. Polished stone axe-heads are still used by native peoples in some of the South Sea islands. It is interesting to find that whereas most Australian aborigines make stone implements in Palaeolithic fashion, some tribes in the eastern half of the continent have learnt to grind the edges of stone axes in accordance with Neolithic custom.

The typical polished stone axe-head was first shaped by percussion flaking (Fig. 13 *d*), and then the cutting edge or

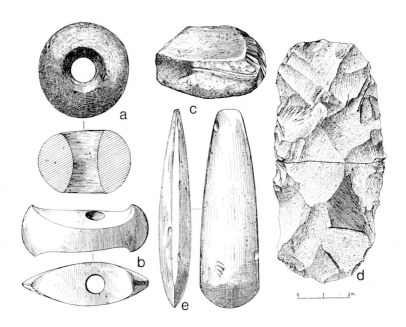

Fig. 13. *Polishing and drilling of stone.* *a.* "Mace-head" of sarsen-stone with hour-glass perforation, Mesolithic, Boreal peat, Southampton. *By courtesy of Southampton Museum.* *b.* Basalt battle-axe with cylindrical shaft-hole Chalcolithic, Denmark. *c.* Sarsen-stone used for polishing celts, Farnham, Surrey. *d.* Joined halves of lava celt broken while being chipped into shape before polishing, Graig Lwyd axe-factory, Penmaenmawr, N. Wales. *e.* Polished axe-head (celt) of greenish-grey volcanic tuff of Stake Pass type, Kelso, Scotland. *By courtesy of C. T. Trechmann.*

the whole surface (Fig. 13 *e*) was ground down by rubbing on a slab of wetted sandstone, or other hard rock (with sand as an abrasive if the rock itself was not friable). Blocks of stone with concavities produced by the grinding of axes have been found on Neolithic and Bronze Age sites (Fig. 13 *c*). Some polished axe-heads, particularly those for ceremonial purposes, for example the vivid green jadeite axe-heads buried with Neolithic and Bronze Age chiefs in Brittany and elsewhere, show such a high polish that it seems probable that they were burnished by rubbing with skin and polishing powder.

Stone celts were hafted in various ways (Figs. 7 b, 40 d, e). Occasionally in Mesolithic times, and commonly in the Neolithic and Bronze Ages, certain types of stone axe-heads, hammers and mace-heads were made with a perforation to take the shaft. The earliest examples of shaft-holes in stone are hour-glass shaped, which indicates that they were made by pecking or drilling alternately from both sides of the stone until the two conical pits met and formed a perforation. Discs of quartzite or other fine-grained rock bored in this way have been found on many prehistoric sites. In Europe the earliest examples of these bored stones are Mesolithic (Fig. 13 a) or even late Palaeolithic. Some may have been used as hammer- or mace-heads, especially in later periods; but in South Africa they were primarily used by Bushmen as weights for digging-sticks (Fig. 40 f, g).

The cylindrical shaft-holes of the Late Neolithic and Bronze Age axe-heads and hammer-heads were evidently made with a rotary and in some cases tubular drill, presumably operated with a bow. The concave surfaces of the earliest known battle-axes (Chalcolithic), mostly of diorite or basalt (Fig. 13 b), were probably produced by using a flint rubbing-stone in combination with sand and water.

Where the material was suitable the technique of hammer-dressing was sometimes employed to shape mace-heads and other stone tools and weapons requiring round surfaces (Figs. 13 a, 35 f).

6. Outline of the Cultural Sequence in Relation to Geology

In writings on the Stone Age two words are frequently used in a rather special sense—"industry" and "culture". The sum total of what a particular human society practises, produces and thinks may be called its culture. The culture of a prehistoric society is known solely by its durable products, for example, stone artifacts. Any set of artifacts which is evidently the work of a single human group is said to constitute an *"industry"*. Thus, the stone hand-axes found at St Acheul form an industry; those found at Hoxne another; both representing the Palaeolithic culture now named Acheulian.

The succession of prehistoric cultures in any particular region is worked out by studying the stratigraphy of the deposits containing their industries. Those of the earliest periods, with which we are here concerned, are mainly stone or bone implements, and they are found chiefly in deposits spread by rivers or accumulated in lakes and in caves and rock-shelters and sometimes in deposits of wind-borne dust or sand.

The oldest Stone Age industries, consisting of pebble-tools, hand-axes, or primitive flake-tools, and cores, are grouped as EARLY, or LOWER PALAEOLITHIC. In Europe they are found mainly in ancient river gravels, and for that reason the older Palaeolithic era, covering more than three-quarters of human prehistory, used to be called the River Drift period.

Rivers, as they meander to and fro across their alluvial flood-plain, lay down gravels, sands and loamy clays (brickearths), but when they cut their valleys deeper, patches of these deposits are left in terraces along the valley-sides. Briefly, terraces are the result of the process of valley-deepening having been interrupted at intervals by valley-silting, or aggradation, but in detail the story is complex (see Fig. 14).

In their lower reaches, rivers were affected during the Pleistocene by changes of sea-level. During the maxima of glaciations so much water was locked up in the form of ice on the land that the sea-level sank, possibly by as much as 300 feet. The increased fall to the sea gave the rivers greater erosive power, and they cut their valleys deeper. This down-cutting began at the mouth and worked upstream. During the interglacial periods, on the other hand, sea-level rose and rivers became more sluggish and built up thick deposits. Changes of sea-level were not immediately registered in the upper reaches of long rivers, where alteration in volume of water due to climatic changes was the factor mainly controlling erosion and aggradation.

Alternate erosion and deposition in river valleys would not account for a series of terraces unless on balance down-cutting had been in excess of aggradation. Since all the larger rivers of the world show a series of terraces extending to the region of their mouths, and corresponding to raised beaches

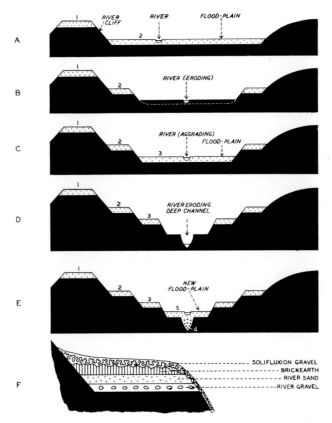

Fig. 14. *Formation of river terraces.* A–E: Stages in evolution of valley (1 = plateau gravel, relic of some older river system; 2–5 = successively younger river deposits, 2, 3, and 5 forming terraces, 4 occupying a "buried channel") F: Section through typical river terrace in north-west Europe, showing stratification.

around the coasts, it is probable that, superimposed on the up-and-down movement of sea-level due to glaciation and deglaciation, there has been a continual fall of mean sea-level relative to the land-masses.

The surfaces of the main terraces of the Thames are approximately 10 ft, 25 ft, 50 ft, 100 ft and 150 ft above the present river-level. Below the river bed there is a buried channel which was cut by the river when the sea had sunk below its present level during the last glaciation, and subsequently filled with gravels and alluvium. Although as a rule the stratified deposits on a low-level terrace are younger than those on a higher one, a low terrace sometimes includes patches of deposit laid down in a deep channel broadly contemporary with, or antedating the deposits found on the terrace above.

Within a particular terrace the lower layers of river deposit have of course been laid down before the upper (this is the principle of stratification—see Fig. 14F). In the famous section of the 100-ft. terrace of the Thames at Swanscombe, near Dartford, the Lower Gravel yields a primitive flake industry known as Clactonian, while the Middle Gravels contain hand-axes representing Acheulian culture. The deposits forming the next terrace at lower level (the 50-ft. terrace) contain flake implements of a type called Levalloisian, together with rolled and derived examples of the Clactonian and Acheulian industries. Thus, locally at any rate, the cultural sequence was Clactonian, Acheulian and Levalloisian. Studies of similar sequences in other areas have shown, however, that the general succession of cultures in north-west Europe was more complex, that an earlier Acheulian elsewhere preceded the Clactonian of Swanscombe, that a later Acheulian elsewhere succeeded the earliest Levalloisian; and so on.

It appears that in Europe there were two parallel lines of Early Palaeolithic culture. In the one called Acheulian, undoubtedly of African origin, bifacial core-tools (hand-axes) predominated (p. 42); in the other, Clactonian-Mousterian, perhaps of Asiatic origin, flake-tools predominated (pp. 50–6). The Levalloisian (p. 52) is generally classed as a "flake-culture", but there are indications that it may represent a tradition of mixed origin. In fact recent discoveries are tending to modify the hard and fast differentiation of flake- and core-tool cultures.

Geologists have endeavoured to refer the various stages of cultural development to the chronological framework provided by the periodic advances and retreats of ice in north-west Europe and central Asia (and similarly in southern Asia and Africa, by the corresponding alternation of wet and dry periods), but no detailed correlations on these lines can yet be made which are free from doubt. It appears that during the second and third interglacial periods hunters using hand-axes roamed widely over north-west Europe, but that during the succeeding glacial episodes they retreated south *or changed their habits*, for they were then largely replaced in France and southern Britain by hunters using flake-tools, who were presumably better adapted to the severe climatic conditions prevailing around the ice-sheets. In Europe east of the Rhine flake-cultures predominated throughout Early Palaeolithic times.

Although man did not penetrate into the ice-covered regions, he frequented the tundra which bordered them, and his implements are therefore sometimes found in the "periglacial" deposits. Under tundra conditions subsoil becomes disintegrated by deep freezing, and during seasonal thaws, or when mild conditions set in, it flows down sparsely vegetated slopes as a semi-frozen sludge, which accumulates as an unstratified deposit, for instance, in the bottoms of valleys. Where the subsoil was Chalk, solifluxion in Pleistocene times produced the deposit known in England as Coombe Rock.

In the Early Palaeolithic, certain groups of men occasionally made use of caves (*e.g.* Pekin Man), but towards the end of that period, when Mousterian culture flourished (sometimes distinguished as MIDDLE PALAEOLITHIC), and during the succeeding period, the UPPER, or LATE PALAEOLITHIC, cave-dwelling became common practice in the limestone regions of Europe, probably as an adaptation to the severe climatic conditions associated with some phases of the fourth glaciation. The "Middle Palaeolithic" (really a cultural, not a chronological term) has sometimes been called the Early Cave Period and the Upper Palaeolithic the Later Cave Period. Whereas the industries grouped as Mousterian consist mainly of well-made flake-tools, those classed as Upper Palaeolithic† (p. 58) are distinguished by the predominance of tools made from narrow blades of stone,

† By convention the term Upper Palaeolithic is applied only to blade-tool cultures. Contemporary cultures based on earlier traditions (*e.g.* in South Africa) are called by the more comprehensive term Late Palaeolithic.

and by the extensive use of bony materials. Much of our knowledge of these later Palaeolithic cultures has been obtained by excavation in caves and rock-shelters.

The deposits on the floors of caves generally include cave earth, mainly clayey matter washed into the cave by infiltrating water; rubble and breccia due to roof falls; and layers of travertine or stalagmite formed by the evaporation of hard water occasionally rising as a spring and flooding the floor, or regularly dripping from the roof. In caves and rock shelters which have been occupied from time to time by prehistoric man these natural deposits alternate with

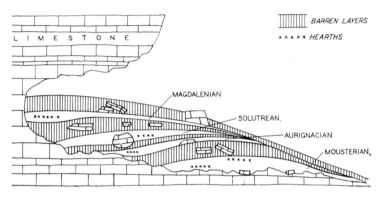

Fig. 15. *Stratification in cave deposits.* Diagrammatic section of ideal rock-shelter (shallow cave, or *abri*), *e.g.* in SW France.

occupation layers, consisting usually of the ashes of fires, food debris in the form of broken animal bones, and artifacts. Systematic excavation of such cave deposits, layer by layer, reveals the changes and substitutions of culture which have taken place in the course of time (Fig. 15). By comparing the sequences in a series of different caves, it has been possible to establish the general succession of Upper Palaeolithic cultures in Europe. The main cultural groups, named after localities in the south of France where they were first recognized, are in order of their appearance: 1, Aurignacian; 2, Solutrean; 3, Magdalenian.†

† For explanation of these and similar terms, see p. 91.

Many provincial variants have now been distinguished, and the term Aurignacian is used in a restricted sense (see p. 59). Under some climatic phases, perhaps seasonally, Upper Palaeolithic man lived in the open. In Moravia, for instance, "Aurignacian" camp sites have been found in the open below deposits of loess (mainly dust blown from the barren periglacial regions), and in France remains of Solutrean culture are found both in caves and on "open sites".

The cultures of the later Stone Age hunters living in Europe and Asia immediately after the main retreat of the ice of the last glaciation are grouped as MESOLITHIC. The industries of this period, recognizable mainly by the presence of microliths (at one time called "pigmy-flints"), are found sometimes in the sandy soil of heathlands, sometimes under peat or river alluvium, or in coastal deposits. Mesolithic peoples appear to have lived mainly by fowling, fishing, and gathering molluscan shell-fish (p. 89). The Danish shell-mounds, or "Kitchen-middens", belong to this period. As the sea-level was rising rapidly in early postglacial times, the industries of the shore-dwelling tribes are sometimes found below tide-mark, for example, in association with submerged forests. In parts of Scandinavia, however, land which had been pressed down by the ice during the glacial period was at this time rising again, so that shore-dwelling sites of Mesolithic age are now above sea-level. Several partly contemporary cultures can be recognized, including the Tardenoisian (characteristic of sandy scrub-land), the Azilian and Maglemosian (in forest environ-ments), the Ertebølle, or "Kitchen-midden" culture, the Obanian, and the Asturian, practically confined to shore-lines.

The final and shortest phase of the Stone Age, called the NEOLITHIC (p. 90), was distinguished by the introduction of agriculture and the domestication of animals as a source of food; by the construction of villages; by the use of polished stone axe-heads, and after a time by the regular making of pottery; and in some regions by the building of megalithic tombs or barrows and the systematic mining of flint. Remains of this phase of culture may be found below the soil, or under recent alluvium or peat, and occasionally in the beds of lakes. The earlier of the prehistoric lake-villages in Switzerland are Neolithic.

7. Evolution of Palaeolithic Cultures

The classification of the oldest or Palaeolithic cultures is mainly based on the succession of stone industries found in north-west Europe, notably in France, where the early researches were carried out. Now that detailed studies have also been made in other parts of the Old World, it is possible to present a general picture of the evolution of culture in Palaeolithic times.

a. Pebble-tool Cultures

The earliest known stone implements are rather simply flaked pebbles and cobbles of quartzite or lava occurring

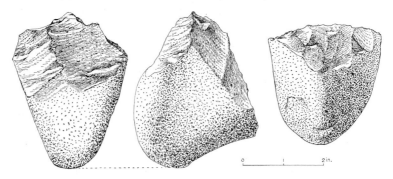

Fig. 16. *Pre-Chellean tools.* Oldowan pebble-tools (lava), Bed I, Oldoway (Olduvai) Gorge, Tanganyika.

in deposits of Pliocene age in north-east Africa. It is probable that some of those found in the part of the Omo Valley lying in Ethiopia come out of deposits as much as 4 million years old. However, the specimens which at the time of writing count as the oldest undoubted works of man are pebble-tools and flakes found by Mr Richard Leakey in 1969 in water-laid volcanic tuffs at East Rudolf, Northern Kenya, dated by their radiogenic argon as 2·6 million years old, that is to say Upper Pliocene according to the classification adopted here.

At one time many archaeologists believed that the oldest implements were those called KAFUAN, small slabs of rock or pebbles flaked in one direction only and occurring in high-level river gravels in Uganda and elsewhere in central and South Africa; but it has now been proved that pebbles are chipped in exactly the same way when gravel cascades over river cliffs. Thus the "Kafuan" is now discounted as an acceptable industry, although it may well be that some pebble-tools described by earlier writers under this name are in fact primitive examples of the Oldowan culture now to be described.

The oldest acceptable stone implements are pebbles, boulders or cobbles flaked usually in two directions to form a sharp edge suitable for cutting, chopping or scraping. This culture is typically represented by large numbers of specimens occurring in the series of lake deposits which comprise Bed I in a thick series of variable sediments exposed in the Olduvai Gorge cutting across the Serengeti Plain in Tanzania. The industry has been named OLDOWAN after Oldoway the name by which the Germans knew Olduvai. The basal layers of Olduvai Bed I have been dated by their potassium/argon ratio as 1·75 million years old, indicating that they belong to the Lower Pleistocene. It is worth noting that the stone tools from the Pliocene deposits at East Rudolf belong to the same culture, indicating that a well defined tradition involving primitive skills remained unaltered among the first men or hominids for hundreds of thousands of years.

The Oldowan industry includes more than a dozen types of tool. In her thorough description and analysis, Dr Mary Leakey points out that although it shows the tool-forms characteristic of a "pebble-tool" industry, in fact the majority of the implements in Olduvai Bed I have not been made from pebbles in the strict sense but from natural cobbles of rock. These were converted mainly into choppers by skilful flaking in two directions at one end or along one side. Sometimes the cobbles were flaked more extensively to form polyhedrons, spheroids, discoids or even crude bifaces (see below). Simple primary flakes were also used as implements, being trimmed for use as points or scrapers. It is remarkable that this oldest human industry included "tools to make tools" e.g. hammerstones and anvil-stones, indicating much forethought. Both at East Rudolf and Olduvai flakes which had been detached in re-sharpening old tools have also been recognized. At a few of the occupation sites in Olduvai Bed I, unmodified cobbles had evidently been transported from elsewhere ("manuports"); in one case loosely piled as if to fix or support skins for a wind-break or shelter.

Pebble-tool industries are now recognized as representing the basic stone-tool-making tradition of mankind, which originated in central Africa during the Pliocene period between 5 and 3 million years ago. This tradition had spread throughout the continent of Africa before the end of the Lower Pleistocene. Rare outposts of pebble-tool culture probably occurred in Europe (*e.g.* Southern France) and South West-Asia, but the evidence so far is unsubstantial.

Pebble-tools are sometimes found along with more elaborate tools in later industries. The occurrence of isolated pebble-tools is therefore no proof of the early age of the containing deposit. Where the most easily available stone for making into tools consisted of pebbles some later Palaeolithic and Mesolithic cultures produced "pebble-tool" industries (*e.g.* Pontinian facies of Italian Mousterian, and Asturian industries in Mesolithic kitchen-middens of Spain).

b. Hand-axe Cultures

Later or Developed Oldowan assemblages included a substantial proportion of pebbles or cobbles which had been flaked all round their periphery, first in one direction and then in the other, so that they became two-faced lumps (*bifaces*), roughly oval or pear-shaped in outline with a sinuous or zig-zag margin formed by the intersection of the flake-scars. These tools led to the invention of the hand-axe, a much more skilfully made implement than any of those in the early pebble-tool industries. Pebble-tool culture had endured for several million years and spread throughout Africa. The hand-axe culture supplanted it in all parts of that continent and then in a comparatively short space of time had been carried by an early species of *Homo* into a large part of Europe and south-west Asia.

In Europe the hand-axe industries are almost invariably made in *flint*. In France the earliest of these was named Abbevillian, but most archaeologists now group all the hand-axe industries as representing the ACHEULIAN culture

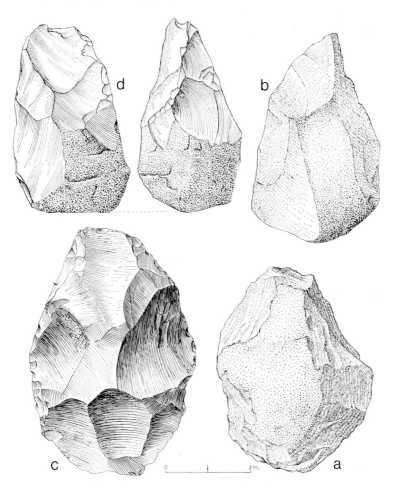

Fig. 17. *Miscellany of bifaces.* *a.* Developed Oldowan biface (formerly "Chellean") made in lava, Bed II, Olduvai Gorge, Tanzania. *b.* Early Acheulian hand-axe in quartzite, raised-beach, Morocco. *After Neuville & Ruhlmann.* *c.* Acheulian hand-axe in flint (formerly "Chellean"), Chelles-sur-Marne. *After Breuil.* *d.* Middle Acheulian hand-axe made from nodule of flint, Caversham, Berks. *By courtesy Oxford University Museum.*

which arose in Africa about 500,000 years ago, reached Europe when the second or Mindel glaciation of the Alps was beginning to develop, and lasted for several hundred

43

thousand years, in fact until the onset of the last or Würm glaciation. In Africa, Asia and Europe hand-axes coarsely flaked with zig-zag margins and of relatively early date have until recently been classified as Chellean (Fig. 17c), but this term, like the better-defined Abbevillian, is being discontinued. All Acheulian industries include a proportion of roughly-made hand-axes, perhaps unfinished pieces or "rough-outs", and these have sometimes been identified rather misleadingly as of "Chellean type". The true precursors of the Acheulian were the crudely fashioned *bifaces* found in the Developed Oldowan (Fig. 17a).

The most characteristic Acheulian hand-axes (Pl. I; Figs. 17a, b, 18, 19, 32), are almond-shaped, oval or roughly triangular *bifaces* with relatively straight margins as seen in profile (Figs. 18a, 32). Their surfaces are formed by shallow, skimming flake-scars. On the basis of experiments many archaeologists believe that such refined flaking can only be achieved by means of a hardwood baton or cylindrical bone. Some coarsely-flaked hand-axes show less evidence of this so-called wood-, or cylindrical-hammer technique, and these may have been shaped by means of a hammerstone.

The hand-axe (*boucher*, *biface* or *coup-de-poing*) was the first standardized implement; like the jack-knife, it was probably a general purpose tool. Apparently it was not hafted, nor was it primarily an axe in the true sense, but served mainly for cutting and scraping. The pointed variety was probably developed for stabbing and for piercing the hide of an animal as a preliminary to skinning (see p. 13). Although the Acheulians used waste-flakes as occasional tools, and made a number of deliberate flake-tools (in Europe and south-west Asia, sometimes of Clactonian form—see p. 50), it is broadly true to say that the hand-axe was the predominant tool in the equipment of the Early Stone Age hunters of Africa, western Europe and southern Asia, and remained so for several hundred thousand years. Acheulian implements collected from successively younger deposits in any one region show a gradual refinement of workmanship. Cultural development was, however, very slow, and these industries remained practically uniform over nearly one-fifth of the world. Many of the hand-axes dug up at localities as widely separated as, for example, the Cape,

Kenya, Madras and London, are indistinguishable except for their being made of different types of rock. However, the shapes and sizes of Acheulian implements varied to some extent with local conditions, and in a few regions one can detect innovations. Ovate hand-axes with an **2**-twist (Fig. 18*b*) are commoner in northern France and Britain than elsewhere. Where suitable pebbles or nodules were not available, and where consequently the raw material had to be quarried from standing rock, the Acheulians began to fashion hand-axes out of large flakes. By stopping the normal process of trimming a squarish flake into a hand-axe at the stage before the thin wedge-shaped end is removed, a special form of tool with true axe-edge was produced, generally known as a cleaver (Figs. 7*a*, 19*c*, 34*a*). Cleavers are common in the Acheulian industries of Africa, but become less so as these industries are traced northwards through western Europe. In the later stages of Acheulian culture, when thin bifacial hand-axes were in demand, it became the custom, even in the flint areas of western Europe, to chip them out of flakes rather than nodules. Many of the hand-axes in the Swanscombe gravels have been made from flakes.

Living-sites of Acheulian man have been found at Olorgesailie in the Kenya Rift Valley, 40 miles SW of Nairobi. Interleaved with deposits formed at the fluctuating margin of a lake in Pleistocene times are "land-surfaces" with remarkable concentrations of Acheulian cleavers, hand-axes (Fig. 18*a*), and chipped stone balls, associated with broken bones of baboons, wild pigs and zebra. It has been suggested that the stone balls were missiles for killing game (similar polyhedral balls are among the oldest known artifacts found in a pebble-tool industry at Ain Hanech, Algeria). It is probable that simple wooden spears and throwing sticks were the principal hunting weapons throughout Early Palaeolithic times, although pit-falls may have been made for hunting the bigger animals. Judging from the discarded meat bones on Acheulian lake-side camping sites at Torralba, Spain, and at Torre in Pietra, Rome, some groups in Europe hunted wild oxen, horses and even elephants. Possibly families banded together in hunting big game.

The Acheulians lived in open or thinly wooded country,

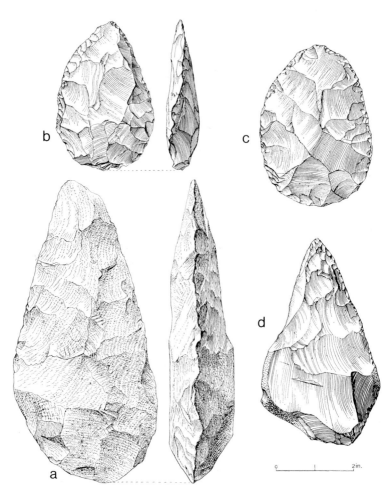

Fig. 18. *Acheulian tools. a.* Lava hand-axe, Olorgesailie, Kenya. *b.* Twisted ovate, *argile rouge* on 30-metre terrace, St Acheul, near Amiens (Somme). *c.* Ovate hand-axe, South of Wady Sidr, Palestine. *d.* Hand-axe, of Micoquian type, brickearth, Hoxne, Suffolk.

and frequented the margins of lakes and river banks. Until the latest stage of their culture they rarely used rock-shelters, and some groups appear to have been without the use of fire (the earliest evidence of its use in Africa is

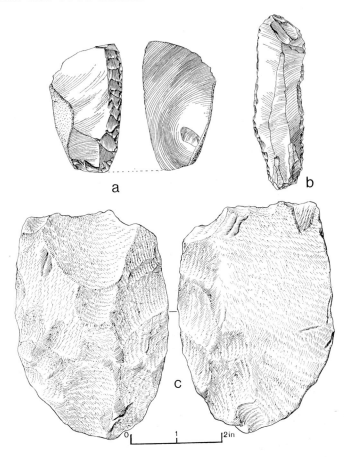

Fig. 19. *Acheulian tools.* *a.* Micoquian flake-tool (flint), Layer Ed, Tabun Cave, Mount Carmel, Palestine. *b.* Utilized blade, gravel terrace of Thames, Lent Rise, near Burnham, Bucks. *By courtesy of A. D. Lacaille.* *c.* Quartzite cleaver from "laterite", Madras, India.

in the Final Acheulian level in the Makapan Cave of Hearths, Transvaal).

Acheulian culture in the developed form known as Micoquian persisted until the early stages of the last glaciation, when it merged into the Mousterian, Levalloisian and the probably related early blade cultures. Before considering these later developments, however, it is convenient to give some account of the flake- and chopper-tool cultures which held sway in the regions north and east of the great hand-axe province.

c. Chopper-tool Cultures

While evidence indicates that man originated in Africa during the Pliocene period, by an early stage of the Lower Pleistocene he had spread into Asia. Early Palaeolithic culture developed along different lines in the two continents. The oldest industry of which we have detailed knowledge in Asia is that found in the CHOUKOUTIEN cave deposits near Pekin (Fig. 31). Described by some as a pebble-tool industry, but by others as a flake-industry, it is really so crude that it could be regarded as basic in type. "*Sinanthropus*", or Pekin Man† evidently collected boulders and weathered pieces of rock from various localities and brought them back to the cave to work into tools. He broke up the lumps by placing them on an anvil-stone and striking them with another stone. Sometimes, no doubt, he found it most convenient to use the resulting flakes, at other times the residual core proved useful. The "*Sinanthropus*" layers yielded chopper-like cores (Fig. 31*a*, *b*), some evidently intentional tools, and large numbers of flakes, some with secondary trimming (Fig. 31*c*). Signs of utilization are difficult to detect on the edges of untrimmed flakes of coarse vein-quartz (which was the material mainly used by Pekin Man), but it is probable that the majority of the flakes were not merely waste-products from the making of choppers, but were intended for use. We have already noted (p. 16) that broken bones were converted into implements by Pekin Man. Judging from the quantities of animal bones scraped or split for marrow, he was a successful hunter, particularly of deer. There is also evidence that he was a cannibal, that he regularly used fire, and that he gathered and ate wild fruits (berries of *Celtis*).

Judging by the type of implement (Fig. 20*c*) found in deposits slightly younger than those with "*Sinanthropus*",

---

† Now referred to *Homo erectus pekinensis*, indicating close relationship with Java Man, *Homo erectus* formerly placed in the genus *Pithecanthropus*.

the Choukoutien industry developed along lines which fore-shadowed the Mousterian (in which the flake tradition was predominant). However, a chopper-tool tradition was also clearly manifest in the CHOUKOUTIENIAN, as in the nearly contemporary Early SOAN of India, the ANYATHIAN of Burma and the PATJITANIAN of Java (Fig. 20). The latter

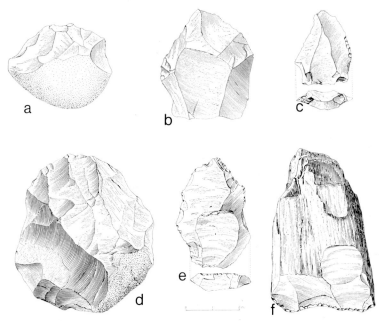

Fig. 20. *Artifacts of Soan culture group.* *a.* Pebble chopper-tool, and *b*, flake-tool, probably of quartzite, Early Soan, NW India. *After De Terra and Paterson.* *c.* Late Choukoutien flake-tool of chert (resembling Mousterian point); Locality 15, Choukoutien, China. *After Pei.* *d.* Chopper-tool, and *e*, flake-tool of silicified tuff, Patjitanian, Java. *After Movius.* *f.* Chopper-tool (hand-adze) of fossil wood, Anyathian, Upper Burma. *After Movius.*

included choppers somewhat resembling the hand-axes of African core-tool tradition, as well as crude Levalloisoid flake-tools. Flake and chopper industries predominated in south-eastern Asia throughout the Pleistocene period. This Soan culture-complex was an essentially Asiatic develop-ment, but had slender connections with the contemporary Palaeolithic cultures of the west.

d. Flake-tool Cultures

Utilized flakes occasionally accompany even the early pebble-tool industries of South Africa, so it is evident that extensive use of flakes may have developed spontaneously in various regions. However, it has been suggested that the primitive flake-industry found in Europe and known as CLACTONIAN (Fig. 21) represents an early off-shoot of the Choukoutien-Soan group of cultures, although similar industries (e.g. HOPE FOUNTAIN) occurred as a specialized facies of the hand-axe industries in South and East Africa. Clactonian knappers were mainly concerned with the production of serviceable flakes. Taking a suitable lump of flint or other stone, they struck flakes from around the sides, first from one direction and then from the reverse direction. The scars of one set of flakes served as the striking-platforms for the next. Clactonian flakes show a wide angle between the bulbar face and the striking-platform, while the bulb of percussion is very prominent (Figs 4 b', 21c are typical). These features suggest that most flakes were produced by striking the lump on the edge of an anvil-stone. Clactonian cores are sometimes chipped all round and are then roughly bi-conical in shape, but more commonly the original surface or cortex of the stone has been retained on one side (Fig. 21a), perhaps to accommodate the subsequent use of the core as a chopper, as in the Soan industries. Suitable flakes were selected and their edges trimmed for use as scrapers or knives. Clactonian industries generally include a fairly high proportion of concave scrapers (Fig. 5), such as would have served as "spoke-shaves" for the shaping of wooden spears (see p. 14). The end of a wooden spear was found in a peaty deposit at the type locality of the Clactonian (Fig. 5).

The manufacture of hand-axes yielded some waste-flakes with Clactonian characteristics, but true Clactonian industries, as found at the type locality and in the Lower Gravel of the 100-ft. terrace of the Thames at Swanscombe, are entirely devoid of hand-axes. Their output consisted of chopper-like cores, and numerous flakes with wide, plain striking-platforms, many with dressed edges (Fig. 21b–d).

There is evidence suggesting that people with Clactonian culture were the first inhabitants of Britain, perhaps entering during a mild interval within the period of the

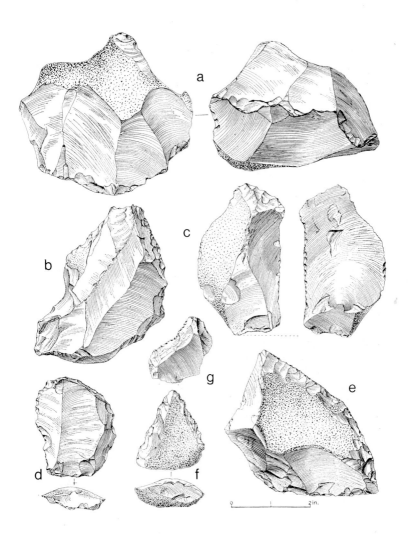

Fig. 21. *Clactonian and Tayacian artifacts.* *a.* Clactonian flint core, and *b*, *c*, flake-tools, Lower Gravel, 100-ft. terrace, Swanscombe, Kent. *d.* Flake-tool, *Elephas antiquus* gravel, Clacton-on-Sea, Essex. *e.* Acheulo-Clactonian scraper, High Lodge, Mildenhall, Suffolk. *f.* Proto-Mousterian flake-tool, Combe-Capelle, Montferrand (Dordogne), *g.* Tayacian flake (utilized), La Micoque, Tayac (Dordogne).

second glaciation. At any rate, judging from the Swans-combe sequence, Clactonian folk appear to have been in sole occupation of the Lower Thames valley during the earlier part of the second interglacial period, after which they became largely supplanted by the makers of Acheulian hand-axes. Locally the Clactonian and Acheulian traditions became inextricably blended, and it is uncertain whether industries such as that found at High Lodge, Suffolk (Fig. 21e), should be regarded as Clactonian influenced by Acheulian, or *vice versa*.

In eastern and central Europe flake-cultures predominated throughout the Early Palaeolithic period, and there the Clactonian (or the closely allied, but as yet rather poorly defined TAYACIAN—Fig. 21 f) probably developed into the Mousterian culture, characteristically associated with Nean-dertal Man. But in some regions, including parts of western Europe where flake-cultures and hand-axe cultures alternated and intermingled, the dominant flake-tradition from the time of the third glaciation onwards was the LEVALLOISIAN (Fig. 22). Its origin and nature are worth considering in some detail.

Towards the end of the second interglacial period in Europe it became the fashion among certain groups of Palaeolithic hunters to prepare nodules of flint in such a way that the form of the flake or flakes to be struck from them was accurately determined. The preparatory flaking aimed at so shaping the nodule that a flake could be detached which would be immediately serviceable as an implement without further dressing. In the commonest form of this fashion the prepared core resembled an inverted tortoise-shell (Figs. 22a, a', a'', 34 b). A suitably directed blow at one end of such a core will split off a flake consisting of part of the more gently domed side. Viewed on its outer face an oval flake thus detached from a tortoise-core has the ap-pearance of a flat, finely worked hand-axe (Fig. 22 b). It is a tool which, combining plano-convex form with thin sharp margins, would obviously be very well suited for use as a skinning knife. The striking-platform of the flake, having been part of the steep end of the tortoise-core, is usually crossed by portions of the preparatory flake-scars. Such a flake is said to have a *faceted butt* (Fig. 22 includes several examples), but a similar effect is produced in striking

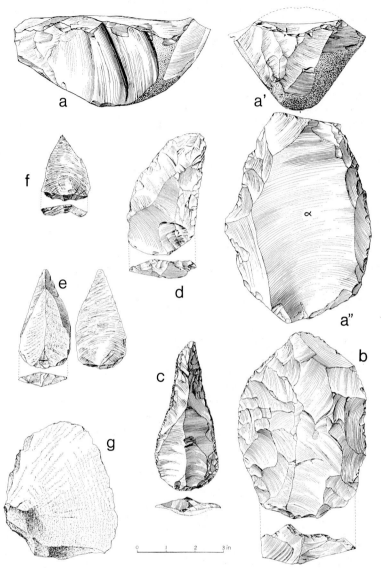

Fig. 22. *Levalloisian and Levalloisoid artifacts.* *a, a′, a″.* Tortoise-core (three views), Baker's Hole industry, Northfleet, Kent. *b.* Flake with faceted striking-platform, similar to the one struck from area α on the above core; Northfleet Kent. *c.* Pointed flake-tool from "floor" in Crayford brick-earths. *d.* Knife-like flake-tool from loess on 10-metre terrace, Montières (Somme). *e.* Pointed flake-tool (chert), Somaliland. *f.* Pointed flake-tool (quartzite), tin-gravels, Darkton, Swaziland. *g.* Faceted flake (lava), Acheulian "floor" Kariandusi, Kenya.

53

flakes from a hand-axe (Fig. 22g), and by secondary trimming of the butt-end of a flake.

Palaeolithic industries consisting principally of flake-tools produced by the tortoise-core technique are usually classed as Levalloisian. The technique was sometimes modified so that, instead of oval flakes, long narrow flakes or flake-blades were produced (Fig. 22c). Some Levalloisian flakes have prominent bulbs of percussion and were evidently struck from the core with a hammerstone (Fig. 9a); but more usually they have rather flat, diffuse bulbs of percussion, due perhaps to the force being spread by the faceting.

As a rule Levalloisian flakes were retouched little if at all, although the butts of flake-blades were sometimes reduced as if for hafting.

It seems that the use of the prepared core technique may have been invented independently by more than one group of Stone Age people. Thus it certainly originated at a very early date in South Africa as a direct development of the Acheulian. The oldest known tortoise-cores are found associated with an Acheulian industry at Victoria West in Cape Province. A struck tortoise-core from this site may be pictured as a modified discoidal hand-axe with one face rather less convex than the other, and from which a flake has been removed, leaving an oval scar with a horseshoe-shaped border. Levalloisoid flakes occur, too, in the Acheulian of East Africa (Fig. 22g). The Levalloisian tradition proper, appears to be of later origin, and according to one view, arose as a result of contacts of the Acheulian people with the Proto-Mousterians. The so-called "Early Levallois" of Western Europe replaced typical Acheulian culture at the time of the third glaciation, just as the Clactonian replaced Early Acheulian during the second; but it is doubtful if the exponents of the new technique were mainly of Mousterian or Acheulian stock. Flake-culture, with its concentration on the production of skinning-knives and skin-scrapers, was more appropriate than hand-axe culture to life in cold or wet climates, and may have been adopted by some of the Acheulian peoples when faced with changing conditions. During some phases of culture, flake-tools of Levalloisian type and bifacial hand-axes (Fig. 23g) were made simultaneously. However, whatever its origin, the Levalloisian tradition persisted strongly in north-west

Plate II

a

0   1   2 in

b

c

1. Material from Palaeolithic (Levalloisian) "floor", Crayford, Kent. *a.* Prepared core (broken before completion). *b.* Waste-flakes, reunited. *c.* Flint nodule reconstructed from the waste-flakes of *a.*

2. Modern flaking "floor": aborigines striking flakes from cores in New South Wales. *By courtesy of Australian Museum.*

Europe throughout the third interglacial period, and during the first stage of the last glaciation; in some regions it lingered on almost to the end of the Pleistocene.

The best known Levalloisian industries in Britain are those discovered at Northfleet and Crayford on the Kent side of the Lower Thames Valley. At Northfleet (Baker's Hole) hundreds of large oval tortoise-cores and flakes with faceted butts have been found under the chalky deposit known as Coombe Rock (Fig. 22a", b).

Crayford is famous in the history of research on the Palaeolithic, for it was here, under waterlaid brickearths of the 50-ft terrace, that F. C. J. Spurrell discovered, about 1879, a "floor" or concentration of flint flakings, representing the spot on the river bank where Palaeolithic knappers had worked. He found lying on a pile of the flakings part of the lower jaw of a woolly rhinoceros, possibly the remains of the knapper's food. The principal products of the Crayford industry were pointed Levalloisian blades, but it is evident that most of the flakes found on the buried "floor" were rejects. Spurrell collected all the chips, flakes and cores revealed by the excavations in the brickearth, and found that some of them fitted together (Pl. II, 1b). He recovered almost every flake which had been removed from one of the cores, more than sixty, and replacing them one by one rebuilt the parent nodule (Pl. II, 1c). The nodule, which had apparently been obtained fresh from chalk-residue, measured about 25 cm. by 15 cm., and had been worked down to a core 9·5 cm. by 6·5 cm. The flint evidently proved of poor quality, for the core (Pl. II, 1a) was found in two pieces, apparently having broken before yielding the blade (such as Fig. 22c) which was the object of the knapper's labour.

The practice of tortoise-core technique ranged widely in space and time. In Africa, where it was used early by the Acheulians, it was adopted by many of the later Palaeolithic peoples, particularly in the so-called Middle Stone Age of South Africa. The arrowheads of the Stillbay culture, for example (Fig. 26e), although surfaced by pressure-flaking, were struck in the first place from tortoise-cores. In Egypt and in parts of Europe and Asia "Levalloisian" methods were still used in Neolithic times, for instance in the flint-mining industry at Grime's Graves in Norfolk.

The MOUSTERIAN represents the material culture of Neandertal Man, and has been found at many localities in Western Asia, Europe and North Africa. It developed out of the Clactonian group, but was influenced by Acheulian and Levalloisian traditions. The typical Mousterian industry (Fig. 23*a–d*) occurs at two levels in the rock-shelter at Le Moustier in the Dordogne, separated from one another by a thick zone containing an industry of hand-axes (Fig. 23*f*) and flake-tools, known as *Moustérien à tradition acheuléenne*. Levalloisian technique was used here to some extent throughout, but not in the Mousterian industries of the type found at La Quina (Charentian) which show stronger Clactonian tradition. The Mousterian industries of Kent's Cavern (Fig. 23*g*, *h*), and of La Cotte de St. Brelade, Jersey, include hand-axes and flake-tools struck from prepared cores. (The term Mousterian has also been widely used in older literature for industries which would now be classified as Clactonian or Levalloisian.)

The earliest Neandertalers with Mousterian culture, such as those of Ehringsdorf, near Weimar, lived under the warm conditions which prevailed in Europe during the latter part of the third interglacial period, and their mode of life was similar to that of the Acheulians. The later or typical Mousterian culture developed in Europe under the cold tundra conditions associated with the first stage of the fourth glaciation. The Neandertalers adapted themselves to the severe climate by using caves as dwellings where possible, and probably by wearing animal pelts. They made regular use of fire, and no doubt this helped in driving away the fierce carnivores which during the Ice Age competed with man for the occupation of caves.

As regards material equipment the Neandertalers showed little more inventiveness than the Early Palaeolithic peoples. They do not appear to have mastered the craft of working bone, although they broke the long bones of animals for use as tools (Fig. 9 *d*), and selected dense bones, such as the phalanges of bison, for service as chopping blocks or anvils. Typical Mousterian industries include small discoidal cores and two main types of flake-tool, usually with plain striking-platforms and finely retouched edges: the side-scraper (Fig. 23*a*, *b*), sometimes D-shaped, and the triangular point (Fig. 23 *d*), with one or both edges dressed for use as a

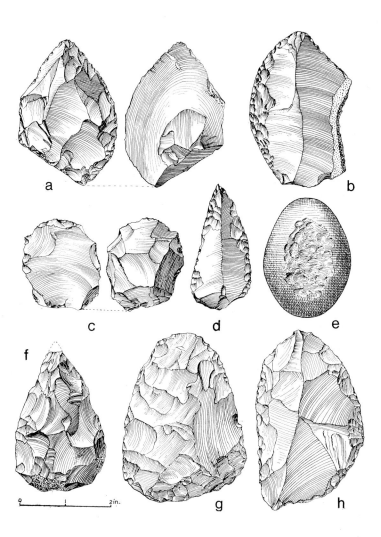

Fig. 23. *Mousterian industries. a, b.* Side-scrapers (*râcloirs*). *c.* disc-core, and *d,* point, from rock-shelter at Le Moustier near Peyzac (Dordogne). *e.* Small anvil- or hammerstone (pebble of ferruginous grit), Gibraltar caves. *f.* Hand-axe from Le Moustier. *g.* Hand-axe (chert), and *h,* oval flake-tool (flint), from Kent's Cavern, Torquay. *a–d.* Typical Mousterian; *f, g, h.* Mousterian of Acheulian tradition.

57

knife. The flake-tools were no doubt used principally for skinning and cutting up animals killed in the hunt, and for preparing pelts. Neandertalers were remarkably fearless and proficient hunters, for they successfully hunted mammoth and rhinoceros. Their weapons included wooden spears (see p. 14), but the round balls of limestone found in the cave of La Quina (Charente) suggest that these people sometimes used stone missiles. Discarded meat bones, many of them broken and split lengthwise for marrow, and some of them burnt, are common in Mousterian occupation layers. From the abundance of limb bones and the rarity or absence of ribs and vertebrae, it appears that when the Mousterian hunters had a successful kill they did not drag the whole carcass to the cave-dwelling, but cut it up on the spot and carried away portions.

The Neandertalers were sometimes cannibals, with a predilection for brain; but they had also begun to bury their dead, occasionally at least with some ceremony. A Neandertal skull with the hole in its base artifically enlarged was found within a circle of stones on the floor of a cave in Monte Circeo, Italy. The body of the man of La Chapelle aux Saints had been buried in a small rock-shelter, selected for the purpose, together with fine implements and portions of bison.

e. Blade-tool Cultures

The Upper Palaeolithic industries which in many parts of Europe abruptly succeeded the Mousterian (Middle Palaeolithic) tell of extensive migrations and comparatively rapid cultural evolution during the later stages of the last glaciation. The Upper Palaeolithic peoples appear to have been nurtured in south-western Asia and eastern Europe, whence they, or at least their traditions, spread in a series of waves mainly westwards to the Mediterranean and Atlantic seaboards. Northwards, migration was limited by the ice-sheets. Compared with all predecessors, the possessors of the new tradition were remarkably inventive. They made a wide range of specialized tools and weapons, and in environments where wood was scarce they mastered the working of bone and other animal substances. Some had a developed aesthetic sense and displayed artistic skill scarcely excelled in any later period; they decorated their bodies and buried their dead with ceremony. In spite of these and other cultural advances man was still uncivilized, in the sense that he was for the most part a nomadic food-gatherer, unable to live a settled communal life except in times of unusual plenty, because methods of producing food (agriculture and animal husbandry) were as yet unknown to him.

A fairly detailed knowledge of Upper Palaeolithic cultures has been obtained by systematic excavation of innumerable sites in Europe and Asia. It is, however, beyond the scope of this handbook to do more than to indicate the chief features of life in the final phases of the Old Stone Age, and to introduce the current terminology. Despite regional differentiation, all Upper Palaeolithic cultures had certain features in common. Thus the characteristic stone tools were made from narrow parallel-sided flakes (*i.e.* blades), produced by the punch technique (Fig. 11*b*), and included specialized implements called gravers or *burins* (Fig. 24 *d–g*) for engraving or working soft stone, bone, antler and wood. A typical burin is a blade with the sides sliced obliquely at one end so that they meet to form a narrow chisel edge (Fig. 24 *g*). Over 20 types of burin were devised.

The earliest Upper Palaeolithic culture, formerly called Lower Aurignacian, but now known as CHATELPERRONIAN, was already foreshadowed in Acheulian times. Possibly originating in south-western Asia, it had spread to western Europe before the end of the Mousterian, for in France, as in Palestine, there was some mingling of the two traditions. The characteristic tool of these hunters was a knife made from a blade of flint with one edge straight and razor-like, the other curved over to the point and blunted by abrupt trimming (Fig. 24 *a*). It was in France, notably in the Périgord region, that their culture reached its full flowering.

Meanwhile another culture was becoming differentiated in eastern Europe—that of the Cro-Magnons or Aurignacians proper. These people spread westwards, and entering France temporarily ousted the Chatelperronians from some of the caves and rock-shelters which they frequented in winter months. AURIGNACIAN culture ("Middle Aurignacian" according to the older terminology) is distinguished by the introduction of methods of working bone and antler by splitting, sawing and rubbing down. The Chatelper-

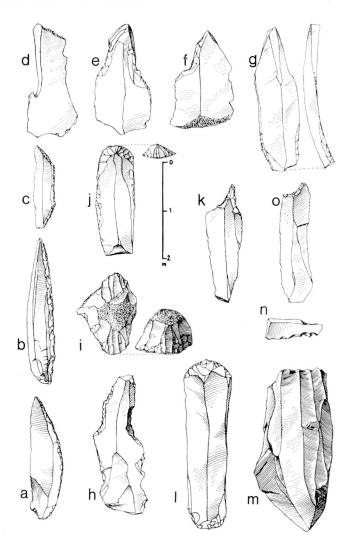

Fig. 24. *Upper Palaeolithic flint tools.* *a.* Chatelperronian knife-point, Châtel-perron (Allier). *b.* Gravettian knife-point, Laussel (Dordogne). *c.* Trapezoid blade, Creswellian, Kent's Cavern, Torquay. *d.* Perigordian (Gravettian) graver or *burin*, Laugerie Haute (Dordogne). *e.* Aurignacoid nosed graver (*burin busqué*). Ffynnon Bueno, Vale of Clwyd. *f.* Aurignacian *burin busqué*, Cro-Magnon, Les Eyzies (Dordogne). *g.* Magdalenian graver (*burin bec-de-flûte*), La Madeleine rock-shelter, Tursac (Dordogne). *h.* Strangulated

ronians (and their descendants) absorbed elements of this
new tradition, and acquired the art of working bone. The
typical Aurignacian "bone" industry includes polished pins
or awls (Figs. 6c, 25 b), and points with the base cleft for the
insertion of a wedge-ended shaft (Fig. 27 f). These latter,
evidently tips for light spears, provide the first good evidence
of a knowledge of methods of hafting. The associated
flint industry includes finely fluted core-like scrapers (Fig.
24 i), end-scrapers (Fig. 24 j), and various edge-trimmed
blades (Fig. 24 h). The earliest known figurative art in
the world is Aurignacian, comprising engravings of sexual
symbols and simple, unsure outlines of animals on loose
slabs of stone. Contrary to views held until recently none
of the art on the walls of caves in France and Spain is
Aurignacian in the restricted sense.

Aurignacian culture was supplanted in western Europe by
the GRAVETTIAN, of which the Chatelperronian was apparently the root-stock—hence in the west these two phases
of culture are sometimes grouped under a single name,
PERIGORDIAN. The distinctive flint tool at the Gravettian
stage (formerly called "Upper Aurignacian") is a narrow
pointed blade shaped like a pen-knife, with a blunted back
edge (Fig. 24 b). The associated "bone" industry is more
limited than that in the Aurignacian.

A comparable culture known as the Eastern Gravettian
developed at about the same time on the steppes of southern
Russia. The Eastern Gravettian hunters followed migrating
herds of game westwards along the corridor of grassy steppe,
with scattered woodlands, which lay between the northern
ice-sheet and the glaciated Carpathians and Alps.

Reindeer, bison and horse were the chief quarry of the
Upper Palaeolithic hunters of Europe, but in southern
Russia and Moravia (Czechoslovakia) the Gravettians
specialized in trapping mammoth, while in parts of eastern
France they hunted wild horse almost to the exclusion of

---

blade, or double "spoke-shave," Aurignacian, Laugerie Haute. *i*. Nosed
scraper, or "push-plane", Aurignacian, Laugerie Haute. *j*. End-scraper
(*grattoir*), Cae Gwyn, Vale of Clwyd. *k*. Solutrean piercer, or "hand-drill",
Laugerie Haute. *l*. Double-ended *grattoir*, Magdalenian, Grotte des Eyzies
(Dordogne). *m*. Magdalenian blade-core, Grotte des Eyzies. *n*. Fragment of
saw-blade, Magdalenian, Laugerie Haute. *o*. Magdalenian concave end-
scraper or "spoke-shave", Limeuil (Dordogne).

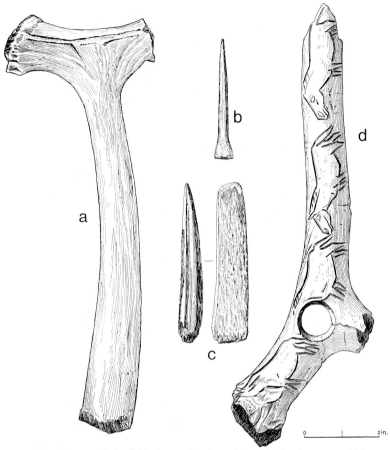

Fig. 25. *Upper Palaeolithic bone and antler tools.* *a.* Antler hammer of Magdalenian age, Moravia. *After Absolon.* *b.* Bone awl of Aurignacoid type, Kent's Cavern, Torquay. *c.* Antler wedge or chisel, Magdalenian, Bruniquel caves (Tarn-et-Garonne). *d.* Decorated *"bâton de commandement"* of reindeer antler, probably as haft straightener; Magdalenian, La Madeleine rockshelter (Dordogne). *After de Mortillet.*

other game. Hunting was probably carried out on a communal basis, judging from the great accumulations of bones on the open-air camping grounds of the Gravettians. On one of the sites found under the loess near Předmost in Moravia, tusks and hip-bones of mammoth had been stacked in separate piles. The mammoths, which were probably

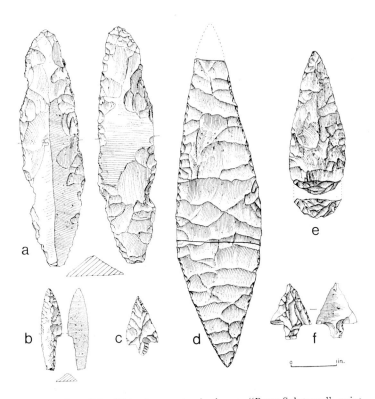

Fig. 26. *Late Palaeolithic stone weapon-heads.* *a.* "Proto-Solutrean" point, Ffynnon Bueno, Vale of Clwyd. *b.* Shouldered "willow-leaf" point (*pointe à cran*), showing pressure-flaking, Solutrean, Fourneau du Diable, Bourdeilles (Dordogne). *c.* Solutrean arrowhead, Parpalló, Spain. *after Pericot. d.* Solutrean "laurel-leaf" blade, or bifacial foliate, Solutré, France. *After de Mortillet.* *e.* Stillbay point (silcrete)—made from pointed flake with faceted butt; South Africa. *f.* Aterian arrowhead, Morocco. *After Caton-Thompson.*

stampeded and trapped in artificial pit-falls, not only formed the main food supply of the Upper Palaeolithic peoples of eastern Europe, but were also sources of various raw materials. Wedges for splitting wood and bone were fashioned from the ivory; the larger bones were occasionally used in the construction of winter dwellings, while dripping from fat-laden limb-bones served to keep fires burning.

The Gravettians, like most Upper Palaeolithic peoples,

were artistic and fond of finery. They decorated articles of
ivory such as bracelets with geometric patterns and they
carved in the round, mostly rather grotesque statuettes of
women in bone, ivory or stone. These Palaeolithic
"Venuses" were occasionally fashioned out of a paste of
clay and powdered bone. The Gravettians (in common
with the Cro-Magnons and Magdalenians) made extensive
use of red ochre, probably on occasion as a body paint,
just as the Australian aborigines and some African tribes
do to this day, and they wore head-dresses and necklaces of
perforated shells, fossils and animal teeth. The earliest
cave art in France and Spain is Gravettian (Fig. 37a, b, c).

During Gravettian times a new culture made its appearance in western Europe, namely, that of the SOLUTREAN
people, who excelled in the art of pressure-flaking, and
similar skilled techniques, applied to the manufacture of
flint weapon tips, including the beautifully made willow-
leaf and laurel-leaf points, or "foliates" (Fig. 26 b, d). These
people, inheriting something of the Pre-Solutrean or
SZELETIAN culture of central Europe, supplanted the
Gravettians in some areas. The decorative frieze of horses,
bison, and ibex, carved in relief on the walls of a rock-
shelter at Le Roc (Charente) is attributed to Solutreans,
who appear to have absorbed something of the artistic
tradition of their contemporaries.

A re-advance of the ice-sheets covering northern Europe
seems to have brought widespread migration to an end, with
the result that the last phase of the Palaeolithic period was
marked in Europe by local variation of a basic culture
which, although of mixed origin, was dominantly Gravettian.
The most vigorous of these variations was the MAGDALENIAN
culture which was centred in south-western France (where it
had begun to manifest itself even before the Solutrean "in-
vasion"), but which diffused its influence over a large part of
Europe.

The material culture of the Magdalenians resembled that
of the Eskimos, possibly because of adaptation to a partly
similar environment. Their flint industry, in the blade-
tool tradition, was skilful and essentially utilitarian, but the
"bone" industry was more elaborate at this stage than at any
other. They made a considerable variety of instruments
in bone, ivory and reindeer antler (Figs. 6 e, 35, 27), in-

cluding spearheads with link-shafts, barbed points and harpoons for spearing fish, "fish-gorges", hammers, wedges and meat adzes, needles with eyes (rare examples occur in Solutrean levels), hooked rods similar to the spear-throwers of Eskimos and Australians, and various other artifacts of uncertain use, such as the "*bâtons de commandement*", first introduced by the Aurignacians, which may have been moulding tools for straightening arrow- or spear-shafts softened in water or steam. They designed these objects with great artistic skill, and on many they engraved lively representations of animals of the chase and occasionally human beings and geometrical designs. Even more remarkable was their mural art (found chiefly in the caves of southern France and northern Spain) which appears to have been a flowering of the tradition begun by the Gravettians of Périgord (Fig. 37). The cave paintings of the early Magdalenians have sometimes been attributed to Gravettian artists because of the similarity of their work, for example some of those at Lascaux, mostly bold outlines and silhouettes. The pigments included black oxide of manganese and red and yellow oxides of iron (ochres). Lumps of pigment were sometimes used as crayons, but they were more commonly ground to powder with pebbles on flat pieces of stone, and then either blown on to greased surfaces of the cave wall or converted into paint by mixing with some fatty medium. Magdalenian cave art culminated in the production of polychrome paintings, with skilful shading to give an illusion of solidity, such as the reindeer at Font-de-Gaume (Fig. 37*j*) and the bisons on the roof of the Altamira cave near Santander, Spain. These versatile people also modelled in clay; for example, the clay bisons in the cave of Tuc d'Audoubert, Ariège.

The subjects of Upper Palaeolithic mural art were almost entirely food animals (reindeer, bison, mammoth, fish, and an occasional reptile or fowl), or animals dangerous to a hunting community (bear, lion). Human figures were sometimes represented, but generally crudely drawn or disguised as animals (*e.g.* the antler-headed sorcerer at Les Trois Frères, Ariège). Paintings or engravings were usually done without regard for previous work on the same wall. Many were done in the dim recesses of caves, as much as half a mile from daylight, usually far from the

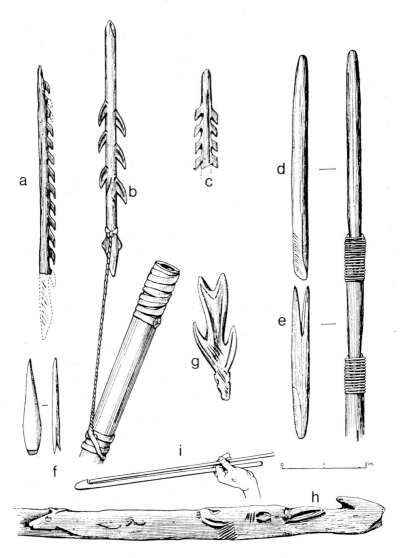

Fig. 27. *Upper Palaeolithic bone and antler weapons.* *a.* Magdalenian barbed point of antler. Bruniquel caves (Tarn-et-Garonne). *b.* Magdalenian harpoon of antler from La Madeleine (*British Museum Collection*), with probable mode of attachment to shaft restored. *c.* Antler harpoon of late Magdalenian type, Kent's Cavern, Torquay. *d.* Magdalenian spear-point cut out of antler (Grotte des Eyzies), and *e*, link-shaft (Morovia), with restoration. *After Absolon.*

dwelling place. The inspiration of many of these cave-pictures was probably the notion that in some way they gave control over the animals portrayed (see pp. 83, 84). The engraving of a bison with spear-points in its side, to be seen on the floor of the cave of Niaux (Ariège), is suggestive of the almost universal primitive belief in sympathetic magic (Fig. 37*h*). It recalls the practice, current in Britain almost to the present day, of sticking pins into wax images of personal enemies. Some of the mural art, however, such as the decorative frieze of sculptured horses in the open rock-shelter at Cap Blanc, near Laussel, suggests totemic beliefs.

It is generally supposed that Magdalenians were nomadic, and that in limestone regions they occupied the mouths of caves during winter and followed migrating herds of game during summer. However, in the Dordogne they were able to hunt reindeer throughout the year. In the grasslands of South Russia the mammoth hunters built earth houses for use at least in winter; in summer they probably used tents or lightly built huts (Fig. 38). Rings of stones marking the sites of skin tents of reindeer hunters have been found near Hamburg. Magdalenians hunted mainly with spears, and judging from some of the cave paintings, they also drove game into traps and snares.

Only stray elements of Magdalenian culture filtered into Britain (Fig. 27*c*), where a contemporary local variation of an aboriginal Upper Palaeolithic culture called CRESWELLIAN was in course of evolution. Many of our limestone caves, such as those in the Mendips, Kent's Cavern near Torquay, Cat's Hole and Paviland on the Gower coast, Ffynnon Bueno in the Vale of Clwyd, and Creswell Crags in Derbyshire, have yielded remains and industries of the Upper Palaeolithic folk of Britain (Figs. 6*c*, 24*c, e, j*, 25*b*, 26*a*, 27*c*).

South-east Spain was occupied during Late Palaeolithic, Mesolithic and even Neolithic times by roving hunters, probably of African origin, who left little material evidence of

---

f. Split-base bone point, Aurignacian, Abri de Castanet, Sergeac (Dordogne). *After Peyrony*. *g*. Forked and barbed bone implement of unknown use, probably "fish-gorge"; Magdalenian, Bruniquel. *After Breuil*. *h*. Antler "spear-thrower", carved with representations of horse and deer, Magdalenian, Laugerie Basse (Dordogne). *After de Mortillet*. *i*. Wooden spear-thrower (*womera*) in use by Australian aborigine. *Not to scale*. *After Brough-Smyth*.

themselves apart from remarkable rock-paintings (Fig. 28). These differ fundamentally from the Palaeolithic paintings of northern Spain and France, and have more in common with the recent Bushman art of South Africa. They are mainly on exposed rock faces, rather than in the recesses of caves; they depict scenes in which human beings are figured as frequently as animals, all in an intensely animated style. A wide range of activities is shown. A common subject is men hunting deer, boar or other game with bows and arrows; more rarely men are seen fighting one another. Women also are portrayed, but, unlike the men, they appear

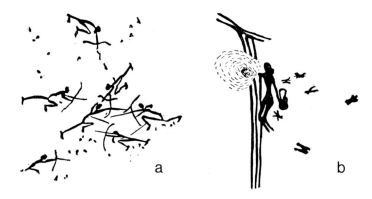

Fig. 28. *Stone Age rock-paintings in eastern Spain.* *a.* Fighting with bows and arrows; red ochre, in rock-shelter at Castellón, × ⅛. *After Hernández-Pacheco.* *b.* Collecting honey on cliff with aid of a grass-rope ladder; red ochre, in cave north-west of Bicorp (Valencia), ×½. *After Obermaier.*

elaborately garbed, and are sometimes standing in groups, as though attending a ceremony. In one scene a person appears to be collecting a honeycomb in a bag—which serves to remind one that before pottery had been invented (in late Mesolithic times), water and liquid food were presumably carried in bags of skin, gut, or bark.

The Upper Palaeolithic people were essentially Eurasian, and until the close of Pleistocene times they failed to affect the aboriginal cultures of the African hinterland. Thus the "MIDDLE STONE AGE" industries of South Africa, dating from Upper Pleistocene times, are mainly Levalloisian, while in the Congo there persisted a derivative of SANGOAN culture in which the place of the hand-axe was taken by a pick-like tool adapted to a forest environment. In parts of North Africa the Mousterian tradition was preserved by the ATERIAN people, who have been credited with the invention of the bow-and-arrow, for they made tanged and winged arrowheads (Fig. 26*f*), as well as small leaf-shaped spear-heads reminiscent of Solutrean forms. They apparently crossed over into Spain during the "Solutrean" phase (Fig. 26*c*).

The blade-tool tradition, however, ultimately spread from

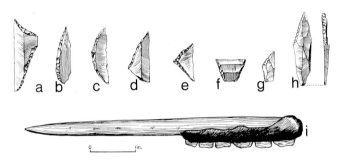

Fig. 29. *Microliths.* *a.* Capsian trapeze ("geometric"), Gafsa, Tunisia. *After Vaufrey.* *b.* Azilian point ("non-geometric") Mas d'Azil. *After Piette.* *c, d.* Capsian lunate and triangle, both obsidian, Kenya. *e.* Triangle of rock-crystal, Bandarawela, Ceylon. *After Noone.* *f.* Tardenoisian trapeze, Tardenois (Aisne). *g.* Tardenoisian point, Ham Common, Surrey. *h.* Mag-lemosian point, Kelling Heath, Norfolk. *i.* Australian saw-knife (*taap*). *After de Pradenne.* For other mounted microliths see Fig. 39*b, g.*

Eurasia to Africa and gave rise to the ORANIAN and CAPSIAN cultures noted for making stone bladelets of regular and often geometrical form (lunates, triangles, trapezes). These microliths (Figs. 29, 39*b, g, h*) were evidently set in a handle or shaft, forming composite tools or weapons, such as barbed arrows or fish-spears. The so-called micro-burin was a by-product of the manufacture of microliths. Stone industries became increasingly microlithic throughout North Africa, Asia and Europe as culture approached the MESOLITHIC phase, when food-gatherers were migrating and adapting themselves to a changing environment. In western Europe, for example, there was a decrease in the average size of the blades produced by the Magdalenians and Creswellians, as their material culture evolved in the direction of the purely microlithic industries known as Azilian, Sauveterrian and Tardenoisian. A similar change affected the Late Stone Age food-gathering cultures of Africa which persisted in places until recent times. The Bushmen of South Africa formerly tipped their arrows with microliths, while Australian aborigines used them until recently, for instance as the teeth of saw-knives (Fig. 29 i).

Fig. 29a. *Mesolithic bow in elm-wood.* Peat-bog, Holmegaard, Denmark. × $\frac{1}{15}$. *After J. G. D. Clark.*

8. Implements Associated with Fossil Man

The skeletal remains of Palaeolithic Man are occasionally found associated with artifacts, more often in cave deposits than in lake- or river-beds; and studies of such associations have made it possible to ascribe the various early cultures to particular extinct species or races of man. These correlations are specially interesting, because it is probable that the mental qualities of the various types of fossil man are reflected more accurately by the implements which they were capable of fashioning than by the structure of their brain-cases.

It should perhaps be mentioned here that the expression "Fossil Man" is generally applied to remains of man of Pleistocene age, that is to say more than 10,000 years old. However, the mere fact of bones being "fossilized", in the sense of having been altered or hardened by infiltration of mineral salts, does not always indicate great antiquity. Thus, a skeleton found embedded in limestone in an island near Guadeloupe (West Indies) is probably not more than a few centuries old. It represents the body of a native buried in a recent beach coral sand, which became cemented by percolation of hard water.

Discoveries by Louis and Mary Leakey in the Early Pleistocene Bed I of the Olduvai Gorge, Tanzania, and by Mr R. E. F. Leakey in Pliocene layers near East Rudolf, Northern Kenya, have left no doubt that the systematic making of stone tools began during the australopithecine stage of man's evolution. There are widely differing opinions about the scientific name most appropriate to these earliest known men who were responsible for the Oldowan pebble-tool culture. They are classified by some authorities

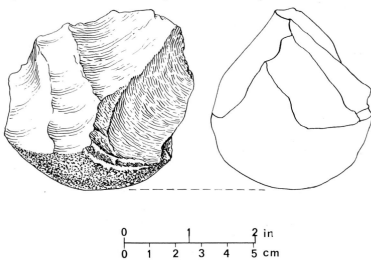

Fig. 30. One of the oldest known implements: *a*. Side-chopper made by flaking a cobble of basalt (cf. other Oldowan pebble-tools, Figs. 16, 33*a*). Found in Upper Pliocene tuffs, 2·6 million years old, containing remains of *Australopithecus*. *After M. D. Leakey.*

as an advanced variety of *Australopithecus africanus* and by others as a very primitive species of our own genus (*Homo habilis*). Judging by the size of the skulls of these men, their brains were very much smaller than any previously counted as belonging to *Homo*. Studies of their leg- and foot-bones show that they were fully bipedal, that is to say that they were able to walk and run in the open on two feet, with the important consequence that their hands were free to make and wield weapons.

Broken-up bones of animals on the "living-floors" of the

Oldowan man indicate that their food included a considerable amount of flesh, some from quite large mammals. It is debatable whether these small hominids were capable of hunting large game, or whether they depended on scavenging the prey of carnivores, which might well have been achieved by skilful group activity.

What has been claimed as one of the oldest human fossils is the mineralized fragment of lower jaw found with pebble-tools (Fig. 33*a*) in the Lower Pleistocene lake-beds at Kanam in the Kavirondo region of Kenya. This jaw-bone has a prominent chin as in modern man, but it has now been shown that the prominence is largely due to a diseased condition of the bone, and that the precise antiquity of the specimen is uncertain. There is no evidence for the view, once widely held, that men with some of the distinctive features of *Homo sapiens* already existed during early Pleistocene times. Indeed, the lower jaws of *"Atlanthropus" mauritanicus* found with Early Acheulian hand-axes and cleavers at Ternifine in Algeria have receding chins and other features indicating membership of the *Homo erectus* group, usually regarded as the earliest stage in the evolution of our genus. The group is represented by the type-specimen (Java Man), by Pekin Man, in Hungary by the Vèrtesszöllös occipital bone found with a refined pebble-tool industry of Clactonian affinity, and in East Africa by the cranium known as H.9 from Upper Bed II in Olduvai Gorge, associated with Developed Oldowan pebble-tools.

No implements were found with the remains of Java Man, neither the earlier form known as *Homo erectus modjokertensis* of Sangiran, or the later subspecies *H. erectus erectus* of Trinil, originally known as *Pithecanthropus erectus*. Beds of slightly later age in Java have yielded the Patjitanian industry (Fig. 20*d*, *e*), which recalls some of the artifacts of the closely related Pekin Man, *"Sinanthropus"*, or in modern terminology *Homo erectus pekinensis*. The Pekin or Choukoutien "Choukontienian" industry (Fig. 31) consists principally of roughly broken pieces of quartz, with a few crudely flaked pebbles of greenstone, quartzite and cherty rocks. As already noted (p. 48), only a small percentage of the pieces are recognizable as tools, but these include chopper-like cores and flakes trimmed as points and scrapers. The industry proved to be practically

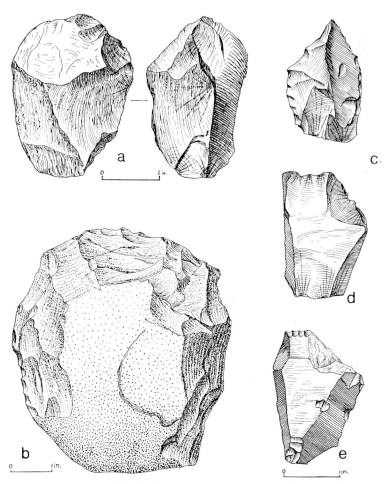

Fig. 31. *Stone tools of Pekin Man.* *a.* Quartz chopper-tool. *b.* Boulder of greenstone flaked into chopper form. *c.* Pointed flake of quartz (compare Fig. 20*c*). *d.* Bi-polar flake of quartz. *e.* Bi-pyramidal crystal of quartz utilized as tool. *After Pei and Black.*

uniform throughout the thickness of the *"Sinanthropus"* deposits, although in the upper layers more cherty rock had been used, and consequently there was a noticeable increase in the number of fairly well chipped pieces. Most

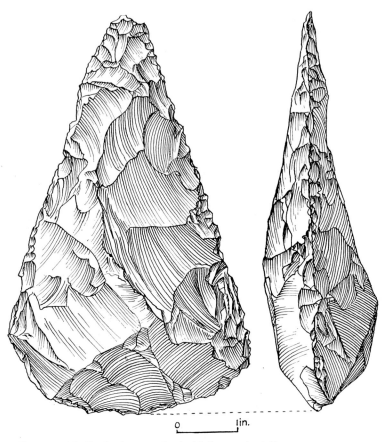

Fig. 32. *Acheulian hand-axe associated with Swanscombe skull.*

of the raw material was evidently collected from the bed of a nearby stream, but crystals of quartz with well-formed facets were found among the tools (Fig. 31*e*), and these must have been sought by Pekin Man in the granite hills some miles away to the north-east or south of the Choukoutien caves.

The earlier chopper-tool and flake-tool peoples of Eurasia were probably all members of the *Homo erectus* stock. The fossil human jaw found in early interglacial sands at Mauer, near Heidelberg in Germany, represents a nearly contemporary but more evolved variant of the same stock, *Homo heidelbergensis.* Animal bones broken as if by design, and resembling the crude bone points associated with Pekin Man (Fig. 6*a, b*), have been noted in the Mauer Sands; also some slabs of sandstone with flaked edges; but none of these is an undoubted artifact.

The evolution of man is difficult to follow in detail because apart from the Pekin material (representing nearly 40 individuals), human skeletal remains of Early and Middle Pleistocene age are very few and fragmentary, for in the earliest stages of culture man did not bury the dead. The evidence at present available suggests that there was more than one line of human evolution.

The portions of a human skull found with Acheulian hand-axes (Fig. 32) in the Middle Gravels of the 100-ft terrace of the Thames at Swanscombe, Kent, are indistinguishable from corresponding bones in some skulls of *H. sapiens*, although exceptionally thick. The Swanscombe skull lacks the frontal region: it may well have had prominent brow ridges like those of the nearly contemporary skull from Steinheim near Stuttgart. The Steinheim skull, and the skulls with a pre-Mousterian or Tayacian industry (Fig. 21*g*) at Fontéchevade (Charente), and with the early Mousterian industry at Ehringsdorf near Weimar, resemble modern human crania more closely than do the large but bun-shaped skulls of the later Mousterian cave-dwellers who were the true Neandertalers (*Homo neanderthalensis*). It appears that these later people, perhaps through being isolated in Western Europe by advances of ice, became modified along aberrant lines and died out. Some of the less specialized Neandertaloids to the south and east, for example, the Mount Carmel people, showed a mosaic of "*neanderthalensis*" and "*sapiens*" characters, and from such a stock either of these species could have evolved. There was not always a close correlation between culture and physical type among early men: thus in the Mount Carmel series the Tabun I skull (predominantly "neandertal") and the Skhul V skull (in which "*sapiens*" characters predominate) were both associated with a Levalloiso-Mousterian industry. The Galilee skull, also Neandertaloid, was found with an Acheulian (Micoquian) industry. Neandertal skeletons of

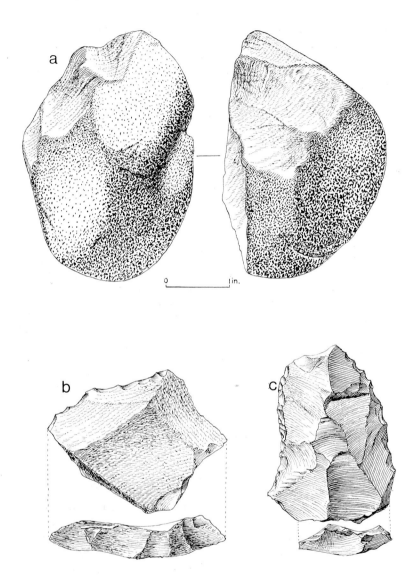

Fig. 33. *Artifacts of fossil man in Africa.* *a.* Oldowan pebble-tool (quartzose rock), Kanam beds, Kenya. *By Courtesy of The National Museum, Nairobi.* *b.* Levalloisian flake (lava) associated with Eyasi Man, Tanganyika. *c.* Levalloisian flake-tool (lava) from beds with Pre-Bushman skull, Singa, Sudan.

Tabun type have been found with Mousterian culture in the Shanidar Caves, Iraq, the latest dated by radiocarbon as about 45,000 years old.

Several other finds in Central and Western Asia have been cited in support of the idea that this may have been the region where *Homo sapiens* emerged. The skeleton of a nine-year-old child, with skull showing a blend of *neanderthalensis* and *sapiens* traits, was discovered in 1938 in the Teshik-Tash Cave in Southern Usbekistan, U.S.S.R. The child's body had evidently been buried with ceremony, for it lay in a grave within a circle of horns of the Siberian Mountain goat. Associated layers of cave deposit contained flint implements of advanced Mousterian types, including flake-blades.

The rapid cultural advances in the Upper Palaeolithic period were due apparently to the emergence of highly successful types of *Homo sapiens*, which spread from south-western Asia at the time when the Neandertalers were dying out in western Europe, around 35,000 years ago. The skeletal remains of the makers of the blade-tool industries have been found at numerous localities in Europe and Asia, and it is evident that already in Pleistocene times *Homo sapiens* had become divided into several distinct racial groups, notably the tall Cro-Magnons (associated with Aurignacian culture), the Předmostians (with Gravettian culture), and the rather Eskimo-like Chancelade race (with Magdalenian culture). There was continual intermingling of races in Europe, with the result that exact correlation between physical type and culture is difficult. Closely related to the Předmostians were the people of Combe Capelle type (Chatelperronian = Early Perigordian) and the "negroid" Grimaldians (with culture of Gravettian affinities). Early races were predominantly long-headed, but there appears to have been a trend towards broad-headedness among some of the Upper Palaeolithic peoples of Europe, including the Solutreans and Creswellians (*e.g.* at Aveline's Hole); and by Mesolithic times broad-headed individuals formed a substantial percentage of the population at some localities (*e.g.* at Ofnet, Bavaria).

The population of Africa during Late Palaeolithic times included various primitive types of *Homo sapiens*, such as the big-brained Boskop race, which probably degenerated into the South African Bushmen of today, as well as remnants of an older stock of Neandertaloids which lingered on in remote parts rather as the "Pliocene giraffe" okapi has survived to this day in the East Congo forests.

The oldest known African Neandertaloid is Saldanha Man, whose skull was found at Hopefield in the Cape Province in close proximity to hand-axes and cleavers of the Fauresmith culture (Fig. 34). In Central Africa, at Eyasi

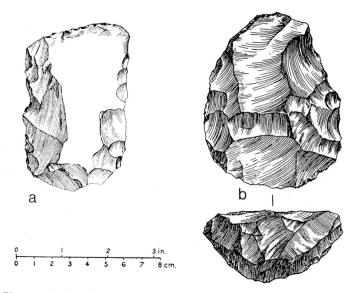

Fig. 34. *Artifacts from site of Saldanha Skull, Hopefield, Cape Province, S Africa.*
a. Fauresmith cleaver in silcrete. *b.* Tortoise-core in silcrete. *By courtesy of M. R. Drennan and Keith Jolly.*

in Tanzania, and at Broken Hill in Zambia, skulls of similar type were found with flake-tool industries in the Levalloisian tradition, locally referred to as Middle Stone Age (Figs. 33 *b*, 35). A re-examination of the material from the Broken Hill "bone cave" has shown that the culture of Rhodesian Man included not only the making of flake-tools from tortoise-cores, mainly in quartz, but also the shaping of bone by grinding, and the production by hammer-

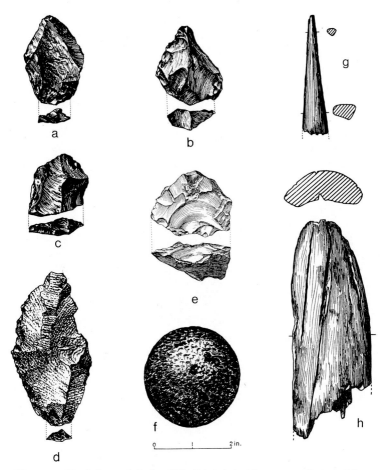

Fig. 35. *The industry of Broken Hill (Rhodesian) Man.* *a–c.* Quartz flakes with faceted striking-platforms. *d.* Flake-blade of quartz. *e.* Disc-core (chert). *f.* Spherical missile stone (granite). *g.* Bone point or awl. *h.* Bone gouge.

dressing technique of perfectly spherical stone balls, perhaps used as missiles in hunting game (see p. 45).

Several skulls in the pre-Bushman group have been found in association with Middle Stone Age industries employing Levalloisian technique (Fig. 33c): the skulls of Boskop (Transvaal), Singa (Sudan) and Florisbad (Orange Free

State). The Florisbad skull was in a peaty bed recently dated by the radiocarbon method as nearly 40,000 years old; from the same deposit fragmentary wooden implements were obtained, possible throwing-sticks. The large-brained Bushmanoid skull from the Fish Hoek cave near Cape Town was from the horizon of the Magosian industry, which developed out of Stillbay culture, and is distinguished by pressure-flaked spearheads made on flakes of Levalloisian type (Fig. 26e). The oldest true Bushman skull is from the Matjes River shelter, in the Cape, where it was associated with an early Late Stone Age industry less than 8,000 years old.

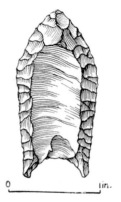

Fig. 36. Folsom point. *After F. H. H. Roberts.*

Aberrant types of man persisted too in parts of southeast Asia, *e.g.* the Neandertaloids found in Late Pleistocene deposits at Ngandong on the Solo river, Java. These deposits have yielded spherical missile stones and a bone industry including a barbed fish-spear.

Human skeletons entombed in the deposits of Late Glacial age have been reported from time to time in the Americas, but in each case the antiquity of the remains has generally been disputed. However, discoveries of stone spear-points (Fig. 36) in intimate association with remains of extinct species of mammals, leave no doubt that nomadic hunters crossed from Asia into North America, presumably by the

Behring Straits, during a partial retreat of ice in the last glaciation but before the extinction of the glacial fauna. Radiocarbon dating of materials associated with these palaeoindians has proved that they had reached as far south as Magellan Strait by 11,000 years ago. There are indications still awaiting confirmation that the antiquity of man in the New World may be at least three times as long as that. The antiquity of man in Australia is probably of the same order of magnitude. At Mungo near Mildura in New South Wales cremation burials were found in association with stone artifacts of the Australian core-and-scraper tradition, and they were dated by radiocarbon as approximately 32,000 years old.

9. Some Attributes of Man the Tool-maker

Tradition and Invention

Men who made tools of standard type such as Acheulian hand-axes must have been capable of forming in their minds images of the ends to which they laboured. Human culture in all its diversity is the outcome of this capacity for conceptual thinking, but the leading factors in its development are tradition coupled with invention. The primitive hunter made an implement in a particular fashion largely because as a child he watched his father at work or because he copied the work of a hunter in a neighbouring tribe. The standard hand-axe was not conceived by any one individual *ab initio*, but was the result of exceptional individuals in successive generations not only copying but occasionally improving on the work of their predecessors. As a result of co-operative hunting, migrations and rudimentary forms of barter, the traditions of different groups of primitive hunters sometimes became blended.

The development of speech, which is generally regarded as one of the chief attributes of man the tool-maker, of course greatly accelerated cultural evolution by facilitating the communication of ideas. The brains of the earliest tool-making Hominidae were probably functionally advanced enough for speech, but nevertheless speech as we know it may have been a comparatively late cultural development—an invention. The earliest mode of ex-

81

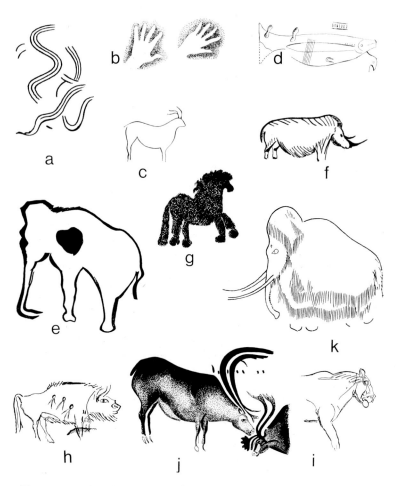

Fig. 37. *Upper Palaeolithic cave-art.* *a–c*, Gravettian, primitive phase; *d–f*, Gravettian, developed phase, *g–k*, Magdalenian.

a. Snake-like scribbles in yellow ochre, La Pileta (Malaga), × $\frac{1}{27}$. *b*. Hands stencilled in red ochre, Castillo (Santander), × $\frac{1}{20}$. *c*. Engraving of ruminant, Pair-non-Pair (Gironde), × $\frac{1}{30}$. *After Daleau*. *d*. Salmon engraved on roof of rock-shelter, Gorge d'Enfer, near Les Eyzies (Dordogne). Note associated bird's head, tally marks (?) and dumb-bell shaped holes, × $\frac{1}{30}$. *After Peyrony*. *e*. Elephant painted in red ochre, Pindal (Oviedo); note heart, × $\frac{1}{18}$. *f*. Woolly rhinoceros painted in red ochre. Font-de-Gaume, near Les Eyzies, × $\frac{1}{20}$. *g*. Horse painted in black oxide of manganese, Lascaux, near Montignac (Dordogne), × $\frac{1}{20}$. *h*. Wounded bison, engraved on floor of cave, Niaux (Ariège), × $\frac{1}{20}$. *i*. Engraving of cave-

pression of ideas was perhaps by gesticulation, mainly of mouth and hands, accompanied by cries and grunts to attract attention. There is no means of proving when speech became general, but the rapidity of cultural change in Europe during Upper Palaeolithic times would scarcely have been possible without the medium of language.

Art, Science and Religion

It would be out of place to consider man's varied cultural attributes in any detail, but the available evidence does suggest that even in relatively early stages of culture man was capable of imagining, deducing from, and speculating about observed relationships between things. Indeed, judging from their art and ceremonial burials, the Upper Palaeolithic races of *Homo sapiens* were capable of abstract conceptions. It is, however, unwise to draw any but the most general conclusions about the ways of thought of "Fossil Man". Upper Palaeolithic peoples, for instance, coated their dead with red ochre, and it is commonly inferred that this was an attempt to restore vitality, the loss of which they are supposed to have connected with lack of redness (blood). This may well be so, but Australian aborigines smear their bodies with ochre on sundry pretexts, especially in preparation for any ceremony; so the Palaeolithic hunters were perhaps merely dressing their favoured dead in the way that they decked themselves for special occasions during life.

The artistic impulse appears to have manifested itself in exceptional individuals long before the Upper Palaeolithic period, indeed probably from the dawn of tool-making. The great Acheulian hand-axe (Pl. I) from the gravels at Furze Platt, Maidenhead, is evidently the product of an artistic craftsman. It has been suggested that a masterpiece of such size and beauty may well have been treasured by the tribe.

Imagination, observation, deduction and speculation ultimately led to art, science and religion, but at first these were scarcely separable from one another. With the reservation noted above in mind, one can illustrate this by considering

---

lion, Combarelles (Dordogne), $\times \frac{1}{20}$. *j*. Reindeer painted in black (male); and in red (female), Font-de-Gaume, near Les Eyzies, $\times \frac{1}{40}$. *k*. Engraving of mammoth, Font-de-Gaume, $\times \frac{1}{12}$. *Mainly after Breuil and associated authors.*

one of the possible origins of graphic art. The earliest known cave art (attributable to the Gravettians or Perigordians) includes wavy lines, silhouettes of human hands and simple outlines of animals (Fig. 37a–f). It is possible that man learnt to draw through the idle amusement of imitating the scratches made by animals, using his hands as stencils, and tracing round shadows with stone tool or lump of ochre in hand. (Even a gorilla has been seen tracing with finger the outline of its shadow on the wall of its cage.) Primitive people are intrigued by shadows. The early hunters would observe that when an animal (or other figure) moves its shadow moves with it, and having a limited range of knowledge, what would be more natural than to deduce that it was part of the animal? By drawing the *imagined* outline of an animal on the wall of a cave, perhaps a Palaeolithic hunter moved by artistic impulses felt that he was doing the equivalent of tracing round its shadow. In thus fixing the shadow—metaphorically—he gained part of the animal, and this he would surely deduce gave him power over it—influencing the increase of the species, or making it easy prey in the hunt. Whatever the chain of reasoning which leads to it, "sympathetic magic" is a kind of primitive scientific theory. It is easy to see, incidentally, how speculation about the intangible phenomena of shadows might have given rise to the conception of spirits, as in primitive religions. Even the civilized ancient Egyptians made special provision in the tomb for a man's double or "shadow".

The art of the cave dwellers provides plenty of evidence of primitive man's keen powers of observation. To mention one example, there is a painting of an elephant on the wall of a cave at Pindal (Oviedo, Spain) showing the animal's heart in the correct position (Fig. 37e)—somewhat reminiscent of the "x-ray drawings" of the natives of Arnhem Land, Australia.

Control of Environment

Through his ability to observe and compare experiences man was able to adjust himself to varying conditions and to modify his environment. Learning to control fire was the greatest step forward in the direction of gaining freedom from the dominance of environment, for through its use man's activities were no longer terminated by darkness, and he was able to extend his range into cold regions. Pekin Man, Vértessozöllös Man and the Neandertalers regularly used fire, and it is therefore presumed that they knew how to make it. It is probable that the first men to use fire collected it from natural sources. Acheulian hearths have been found in Palestine, but none of the meat bones on the living-sites of the same age at Olorgesailie was found to be burnt. Even in recent times some Andamanese and Tasmanian tribes appeared ignorant of how to make fire, and relied on carefully tended fire-brands taken from the fires of neighbouring tribes. It is generally supposed that the Upper Palaeolithic peoples were accustomed to igniting dry fungus by sparks produced by striking iron pyrites against quartz or flint; but fire-making technique may have varied from tribe to tribe. A widely used primitive method is to kindle tinder with the smouldering powder produced when a stick of hard wood is twirled in the hands with its point resting on a piece of dry soft wood. An advance on this is to rotate the stick with a bow, as in the ancient Egyptian and Eskimo "bow-drill". A charred rod of beechwood with one end ground as though by friction was found in a Mousterian layer at Krapina, and has been dubiously interpreted as a fire-drill.

From the predominance of scrapers in some of the Early Palaeolithic industries of Europe, one is inclined to infer that skins were prepared as a means of bodily protection in cold climates, even at very primitive levels of culture. Bone and ivory bodkins and bone belt-fasteners are evidence that the Aurignacians and Gravettians wore skin garments. Judging by their exquisitely finished bone needles (Fig. 6e) the Magdalenians were capable of doing quite fine sewing. The use of rock-shelters and the construction of windbreaks were probably the earliest ways of controlling the environment. In a few of the French caves there are drawings which appear to represent tents and huts, similar to the dwellings of some primitive peoples of today (Fig. 38a–c). Partly underground houses were constructed by the Late Palaeolithic hunters on the Russian steppes (Fig. 38 d).

Control of Food-supply

It was not enough to control physical environment. Man could only advance to civilization by controlling his food-supply. In spite of their high artistic achievements, the Upper Palaeolithic people of Europe were economically no more than food-collecting savages. Their varied culture, betokening a certain amount of leisure, was only possible

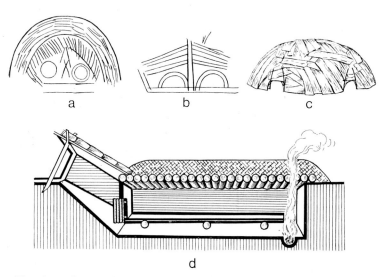

a   b   c

d

Fig. 38. *Palaeolithic dwellings.* *a, b.* Magdalenian paintings of summer huts (?), Font-de-Gaume (Dordogne), × $\frac{1}{12}$. *After Breuil.* *c.* Communal bark-roof hut of aborigines, North Queensland; height 7 ft. *After D. F. Thomson.* *d.* Reconstructed section of underground dwelling (rectangular pit, length *c.* 30 ft, roofed with logs and earth); Upper Palaeolithic, Timonovka, Russia. *After Gorodzov.*

because game was so abundant. Their faith in sympathetic magic must have seemed amply justified so long as conditions of abundance lasted. Family groups of 15 to 20 individuals are normally the largest aggregations having any degree of permanence under a food-gathering economy, but it is possible that the Gravettians, for example, banded together in larger communities for the purpose of organizing mammoth-hunts. Judging from the huge accumulations of mammoth bones on the numerous camping sites of these people in Moravia and south-central Russia, their success as hunters may well have been a factor in the extermination of these slow-breeding animals. With the migration and reduction of game herds, mainly consequent on the climatic

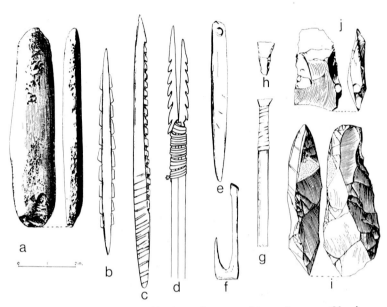

Fig. 39. *Mesolithic fishing and hunting equipment.* *a.* Limpet-hammer, Obanian, Risga, Argyll. *b.* Bone fish-spear with microlith barbs, Maglemosian, Boreal peat, S Sweden. *c.* Barbed point in red deer antler, Maglemosian occupation site, *c.* 7500 B.C., Star Carr, Yorkshire. *d.* Leister prongs of Eskimo fisherman (shows how *c* may have been used). *e.* Net-making needle (?) and *f*, bone fish-hook, Maglemosian, Svaerdborg, Denmark. *g, h.* Microliths (*petits tranchets,* or transverse arrowheads, one found in peat hafted in wood with sinew binding), Kitchen-midden culture, Denmark. *i.* Core-axe with *tranchet,* or transversely sharpened cutting-edge, Maglemosian, Horsham, Sussex. *i.* Flake-axe, Kitchen-midden, Denmark.
a. After Lacaille; b, d–i, after J. G. D. Clark.

changes which brought the Pleistocene Ice Age to an end, the life of Stone Age hunters became precarious.

They had to adapt themselves to new environments, conditioned partly by the rising sea-level, which increased the length of coast-line; partly by the climatic changes which in Europe favoured the spread of forests, but which in parts

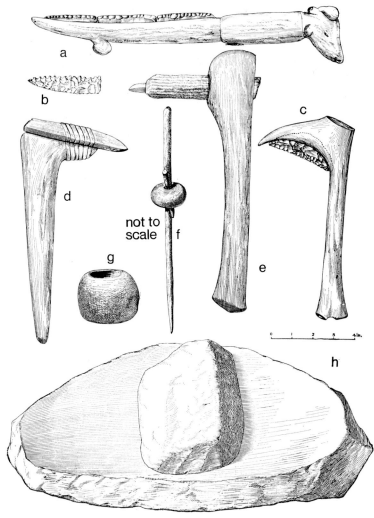

Fig. 40. *Tools of early agriculturists.* *a.* Goat-headed antler sickle with flint teeth restored, Natufian, Mt Carmel, Palestine. *After Curwen.* *b.* Flint sickle-blade, Neolithic, Fayum, Egypt. *c.* Crescentic flint sickle-blade, with haft reconstructed (*after Curwen*), Chalcolithic, Denmark. *d.* "Neolithic" hoe (or adze) with polished stone head restored on basis of contemporary model (Portugal). *e.* Stone adze-blade mounted in wooden handle with antler

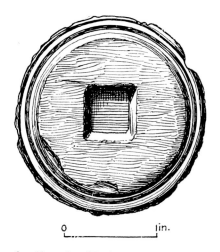

0 |in.

Fig. 41. *Advent of machine-tools.* "Coal Money", a chuck-disc of Kimmeridge Shale turned on Iron Age lathe, Romano-British, Dorset.

of Africa and Asia caused formerly fertile regions to become deserts. Thus migration and nomadism increased. Hunting of land animals was supplemented, in some places practically superseded, by fishing, gathering shell-fish, fowling and sealing. Special equipment was devised for these purposes (Fig. 39). Mesolithic tools and weapons were mainly of composite type, in which microliths were the piercing and cutting elements. The bow-and-arrow was the chief hunting weapon (Fig. 29a). In forest environments, the Mesolothic hunters devised hafted stone axes for working wood. In some localities they made canoes, in the sub-arctic regions they used skis and sledges; and they domesticated the dog. In spite of all these ingenious adaptations and inventions, life remained at the level of bare subsistence until various groups of people in Asia began to adopt the revolutionary practice of cultivating plants and domes-

---

sleeve. Neolithic lake-dwellings, Switzerland. *After de Mortillet.* *f.* A digging-stick such as this (used by food-collecting Bushmen of S Africa) probably served as an early agricultural tool. *After Ratzel.* *g.* Holed-stone, probably for loading digging-stick, East London, S Africa. *h.* Saddle-quern (sandstone), probably Neolithic, Aisne, France. *After de Mortillet.*

ticating animals as sources of food and raw materials. Bone and antler sickles, with flint teeth showing the silica gloss acquired through cutting cereal grasses, have been found on a Mesolithic site in Palestine dating from about 8000 B.C. (Fig. 40 *a*). Within the next two thousand years cultivation of grasses and domestication of animals became well established in the Middle East, whence these practices spread in the Neolithic phases of culture, reaching Britain about 4500 B.C.

The earliest farmers settled near springs, rivers and lakes, and combined argiculture with hunting. Settlements at Jarmo (Iraq) and near springs at Jericho had become towns before 6000 B.C. The Neolithic Egyptians tilled the soil with stone hoes (*cf.* Fig. 40 *d*), grew barley and wheat, which they reaped with flint-toothed wooden sickles. They stored the grain in pits lined with basket-work and ground it on saddle-querns (Fig. 40 *h*), they kept cattle, sheep and pigs, but they fished with hook-and-line, and hunted extensively with bow-and-arrow (indeed one of their flint arrowheads, similar to Fig. 12 *d*, was found embedded in the skeleton of a hippopotamus dug out of dried lake-beds in the Fayum).

By cultivating plants and by stock-raising, and feeding on the natural increase, man had an assured food-supply. The value and yield of plants and animals was enormously increased by selective breeding, so that under the Neolithic food-producing economy not only was a more settled mode of life possible, but larger communities could be supported. Moreover, it was no longer necessary for all members of a community to be occupied in gathering or producing food, with the result that new and specialized crafts developed, mining, basketry, weaving cloth, making pottery—and eventually the working of metals. The rise of civilization in fact followed the introduction of methods of food production, which gave sufficient surplus for the support of craftsmen, scribes, priests, warriors and other specialists.

Under Bronze Age civilization some important mechanical devices were invented (plough, potter's wheel, wheeled vehicle and lathe), and use was made for the first time of non-human motive power, notably of oxen, asses and later horses for traction and transport.

Modern civilization owes its form to machine-tools, driven

by mechanical energy; yet these perform in complicated ways only the same basic operations as the simple equipment in the tool-bag of Stone Age man: percussion, cutting, scraping, piercing, shearing and moulding.

10. Glossary

Stages of Stone Age Culture

Eolithic: Dawn of Stone Age (hypothetical period). Greek ἠώς, dawn; λίθος stone.

Palaeolithic: Old Stone Age. Greek παλαιός, old, λίθος, stone.

Mesolithic: "Middle Stone Age" (Greek μέσος, middle), but better not translated, because in South Africa *Late Palaeolithic* cultures are commonly called "Middle Stone Age", the Mesolithic there being grouped with Neolithic as "Late Stone Age".

Neolithic: New Stone Age. Greek νέος, new; λίθος, stone.

Chalcolithic (= **Aeneolithic**): Transition from Stone Age to Bronze Age (see p. 22). Greek χαλκός, copper; Latin *aeneus*, brazen; λίθος, stone.

Names of Stone Age Cultures

Stone Age cultures have been named after the localities where their industries are well known, or were first recognized, as indicated in the following list. (E.P. = Early Palaeolithic, M.P. = "Middle Palaeolithic", L.P. = Late Palaeolithic (includes "Upper Palaeolithic", a term generally restricted to blade-tool cultures), M. = Mesolithic.).

Abbevillian (E.P.): Abbeville (Somme), N France.

Acheulian or Acheulean (E.P.): St Acheul, Amiens (Somme), N France.

Anyathian (E.P.–L.P.): *An-ya-tha* = inhabitant Upper Burma.

Asturian (M.): Asturia province, N Spain.

Aterian (M.P.–L.P.): Bir-el-Ater, Tunisia.

Aurignacian (L.P.): Aurignac, cave 40 miles SW of Toulouse (Haute Garonne), S France.

Azilian (M.): Mas d'Azil (Ariège), S France.

Capsian (M.): Latin *Capsa* = Gafsa, Tunisia.

Chatelperronian (L.P.): Châtelperron (Allier), C France.

Chellean or Chellian (E.P.): Chelles-sur-Marne, E of Paris.
Choukoutienian (E.P.): Choukoutien caves, 40 miles SW of Pekin.
Clactonian (E.P.): Clacton-on-Sea, Essex.
Creswellian (L.P.): Creswell Crags, NE Derbyshire.
Emiran (M.P.–L.P.): Emireh cave, N end Sea of Galilee.
Fauresmith (E.P.–L.P.): Fauresmith, Orange Free State, S Africa.
Gravettian (L.P.): La Gravette, rock-shelter in Couze valley, Dordogne basin, SW France.
Hope Fountain (E.P.): Hope Fountain, S Rhodesia.
Kafuan (E.P.): Kafu River, Uganda.
Larnian (M.): Loch Larne, Antrim, N Ireland.
Levalloisian (M.P.–L.P.): Levallois-Perret, Paris.
Lupemban (L.P.): Lupemba, Belgian Congo.
Magdalenian (L.P.–M.): La Madeleine, rock-shelter near Tursac (Dordogne), SW France.
Maglemosian (M.): Maglemose, the Great Bog near Mullerup in Zealand, Denmark.
Magosian (M.): Magosi, Karamoja, Uganda.
Micoquian (E.P.): La Micoque, Tayac, near Les Eyzies (Dordogne), SW France.
Mousterian (M.P.): Le Moustier, near Peyzac (Dordogne), SW France.
Natufian (M.): Wadi en-Natuf, Palestine.
Obanian (M.): Oban, Argyll, Scotland.
Oldowan (E.P.): Oldoway (Olduvai) Gorge, N Tanzania.
Oranian (L.P.): Oran, Algeria.
Patjitanian (E.P.): Patjitan, South Central Java.
Perigordian (L.P.): Périgord region, SW France.
Sangoan (E.P.–L.P.): Sango Bay, Lake Victoria, Uganda.
Sauveterrian (M.): Sauveterre (Lot-et-Garonne). S France.
Soan (E.P.–L.P.): River Soan, tributary of Upper Indus, NW India.
Solutrean or Solutrian (L.P.): Solutré, near Mâcon (Saône-et-Loire), SE France.
Stillbay (L.P.): Still Bay, Cape, S Africa.
Szeletian (L.P.): Szeletahöle, Hungary.
Tardenoisian (M.): La Ferre-en-Tardenois (Aisne), NE France.
Tayacian (E.P.): Tayac, near Les Eyzies (Dordogne), SW France.

Tumbian (L.P.–M.): Tumba, Lower Congo basin.
Wilton (M.): Wilton farm, 35 miles W of Grahamstown, S Africa.

11. Selected References to Literature

ALLCHIN, B. 1966. *The Stone-tipped Arrow: Late Stone-age Hunters of the Tropical Old World.* xii+224 pp., 16 pls., 43 text-figs. London.

BLACK, D., and others. 1933. *Sinanthropus* Cultural Remains. *Mem. Geol. Surv. China*, Peiping, (A) XI, pp. 110–36.

BORDAZ, J. 1970. *Tools of the Old and New Stone Age.* xiv+145 pp., 54 text-figs. American Museum of Natural History, New York.

BORDES, F. 1968. *The Old Stone Age.* 255 pp., 78 text-figs. London.

BREUIL, H. 1939. Bone and Antler Industry of the Choukoutien *Sinanthropus* Site. *Pal. Sinica*, Peiping, N.S.D. Vol. 6 iv+92 pp., xxvi pls.

CHILDE, V. G. 1941. *Man Makes Himself.* 4th ed., 242 pp., 11 text-figs. London.

CLARK, J. D. †1950. The Associations and Significance of the Human Artifacts from Broken Hill, Northern Rhodesia. *Jl R. Anthrop. Inst.*, London, Vol. 77, pp. 13–32.

———— 1959. Further Excavations at Broken Hill, Northern Rhodesia. *Jl. R. Anthrop. Inst.*, London, Vol. 89, pp. 201–232.

———— 1970. *The Prehistory of Africa.* 302 pp., 72 text-figs., 48 pls. London.

CLARK, J. G. D. †1954. *Excavations at Star Carr.* 200 pp., 80 text-figs., xxiv pls. Cambridge.

———— †1967. *The Stone Age Hunters.* 143 pp., 137 ills. London.

COLE, S. 1964. *The Prehistory of East Africa.* 382 pp., 60 text-figs., 22 pls. London.

COLES, J. M., and Higgs, E. S. 1969. *The Archaeology of Early Man.* 454 pp., 183 text-figs., 12 pls. London.

CRABTREE, D. E. 1970. Flaking Stone with Wooden Implements. *Science*, Vol. 169, pp. 146–153.

EVANS, J. †1897. *The Ancient Stone Implements of Great Britain.* 2nd ed., 747 pp., 477 text-figs. London.

†These works contain descriptions of specimens in the collection at the British Museum (Nat. Hist.).

GARROD, D. A. E. †1926. *The Upper Palaeolithic Age in Britain.* 211 pp., 49 text-figs., iii pls. Oxford.

———— and BATE, D. M. A. 1937. *The Stone Age of Mount Carmel*, I. xii+240 pp., 8 text-figs. Oxford.

GOODALL, J. 1964. Tool-using and aimed throwing in a community of free-living chimpanzees. *Nature, Lond.,* Vol. 201, pp. 1264–66.

HAWKES, C. F. C., and others. 1938. *In* Report on the Swanscombe Skull. *Jl R. Anthrop. Inst.,* London, Vol. 68, pp. 30–47.

KNOWLES, F. H. S. 1953. *Stone-Worker's Progress.* 120 pp., 24 text-figs. Pitt Rivers Museum, Oxford.

KÖHLER, W. 1927. *The Mentality of Apes.* 2nd ed., 336 pp. New York.

LACAILLE, A. D. †1940. The Palaeoliths from the Gravels of the Lower Boyn Hill Terrace around Maidenhead. *Antiq. Journ.,* London, Vol. 20, pp. 245–71.

———— †1951. The Stone Industry of Singa-Abu-Hugar. *Fossil Mammals of Africa,* No. 2, pp. 43–50. British Museum (Nat. Hist.), London.

LEAKEY, L. S. B. 1953. *Adam's Ancestors.* 4th ed., 235 pp., 34 text-figs., xxii pls. London.

LEAKEY, M. D. 1971. *Olduvai Gorge,* Vol. 3: *Excavations in Beds I and II, 1960–1963.* 298 pp., 121 figs., 41 pls., 10 tables. Cambridge.

LEAKEY, R. E. F., BEHRENSMEYER, A. K., FITCH, F. J., MILLER, J. A. and LEAKEY, M. D. 1970. New Hominid Remains and Early Artifacts from Northern Kenya. *Nature, Lond.* Vol. 226, pp. 223–230.

McCARTHY, F. D., BRAMELL, E., and NOONE, H. V. V. 1946. The Stone Implements of Australia. *Australian Mus. Mem.,* Sydney, IX, 94 pp., 386 text-figs.

MOVIUS, H. L. 1949. The Lower Paleolithic Cultures of Southern and Eastern Asia. *Trans. Amer. Phil. Soc.,* (n.s.), xxxvii, pp. 329–420, 3 text-figs., 4 maps.

OAKLEY, K. P. †1972. Skill as a Human Possession. *In* S. L. Washburn and P. Dolhinow (eds) *Perspectives on Human Evolution,* Vol. 2.

PEI, W. C. 1939. A Preliminary Study of a New Palaeolithic Station within the Choukoutien Region. *Bull. Geol. Surv. China,* Peiping, XIX, pp. 147–87, 25 text-figs.

PRESTWICH, J. †1895. On the Primitive Characters of the Flint Implements of the Chalk Plateau of Kent. In *Collected Papers on Some Controversial Questions of Geology*, pp. 49–80, pls. i–xii. London.

SMITH, R. A. †1948. In *Rhodesian Man and Associated Remains*, pp. 66–9. Brit. Mus. (Nat. Hist.), London.

SOLLAS, W. J. 1924. *Ancient Hunters*. 3rd ed., xxxvi+697 pp., 368 text-figs. London.

SPURRELL, F. C. J. †1880. On the Discovery of the Place where Palaeolithic Implements were made at Crayford. *Quart. Journ. Geol. Soc.*, London, Vol. 36, pp. 544–48, pl. xxii.

WARREN, S. H. †1921. A Natural "Eolith" Factory beneath the Thanet Sand. *Quart. Journ. Geol. Soc.*, London, Vol. 76, pp. 238–53, pl. xv.

WATSON, W. 1950. *Flint Implements*. xi.+80 pp., ix pls., 13 text-figs., 3 tables. British Museum, London.

WYMER, J. Excavations at Barnfield Pit, 1955–60. *In* C. D. Ovey, (ed.). The Swanscombe Skull: A Survey of Research on a Pleistocene Site, *R. Anthrop. Inst. Occ. Paper*, No. 20, pp. 19–61.

12. The Cultural Traditions of Early Man

Australopithecus africanus More than 5 million to 1 million years before present. This tool-using hominid was an incipient tool-maker.

Australopithecus (seu *Homo*) *habilis* 3 million to 1 one million years before present. Displayed regular tradition of making Oldowan pebble-tools and crude bone implements; began hunting mammals such as pigs and antelopes as food, sometimes perhaps scavenged larger game.

Australopithecus boisei ("*Zinjanthropus*") More than 3 million to 1 million years before present. Culture unknown; where associated with stone tools remains of *Australopithecus habilis* or *Homo erectus* also found.

Homo erectus early African varieties included "*Telanthropus*" from Swartkrans, South Africa, and "*Pithecanthropus leakeyi*" from Olduvai (H.9). More than 1 million to 500,000 years before present. Culture: Developed Oldowan pebble-tools and crude bifaces.

Homo erectus mauritanicus of Ternifine. More than 500,000 years before present. Early Acheulian hand-axe industry.

Homo erectus late African variety. More than 150,000 years before present. Late Acheulian hand-axe industry in Olduvai Bed IV.

Homo erectus modjokertensis of Sangiran, Java. Probably nearly two million years old. Culture unknown.

Homo erectus of Java. About 500,000 years before present, or older. Culture unknown.

Homo erectus pekinensis 400,000–200,000 years before present. Choukoutienian chopping-tool industry.

Homo erectus (seu *sapiens*) *palaeohungaricus* of Vértesszöllös. *c.* 400,000 years before present. Small pebble-tool industry with Clactonian affinities.

Homo sapiens steinheimensis c. 200,000 years before present. Culture unknown at Steinheim, Germany.

Homo sapiens cf. steinheimensis c. 300,000 years before present. Middle Acheulian hand-axe industry, Swanscombe, Kent.

Homo sapiens neanderthalensis (*Homo neanderthalensis* of some authors). 100,000–35,000 years before present. Maximum development of typical neandertalers *c.* 50,000 years before present. Mousterian and Levalloiso-Mousterian industries.

Homo sapiens rhodesiensis. 100,000–50,000 years before present. Late Sangoan, Proto-Stillbay and Fauresmith industries.

Homo sapiens sapiens. c. 45,000 years onwards in Eastern Europe, *c.* 35,000 years onwards in Western Europe. Until close of Pleistocene period, culture represented by Upper Palaeolithic industries.

Upper Palaeolithic Men:

Combe Capelle. Early Perigordian *c.* 30,000 years before present.

Cro-Magnon. Aurignacian 30,000–20,000 years before present.

Predmost. Eastern Gravettian *c.* 26,000 years before present.

Paviland. Late Proto-Solutrean 18,000 years before present.

Chancelade. Middle Magdalenian *c.* 14,000 years before present.

Cheddar. Creswellian *c.* 10,000 years before present.

INDEX

INDEX